Gardening Secrets

Gardening Secrets

THE NATIONAL TRUST

First published in the United Kingdom in 2008 by
National Trust Books
10 Southcombe Street
London W14 0RA

An imprint of Anova Books Company Ltd

ISBN 9781905400355

A CIP catalogue for this book is available from the
British Library.

10 9 8 7 6 5 4 3 2 1

Printed and bound by Craft Print Ltd, Singapore.

Text printed on Munken Cream paper which is FSC
accredited from a traceable and sustainable source.

This book can be ordered direct from the publisher
at the website www.anovabooks.com, or try your
local bookshop. Also available at National Trust shops.

Contents

Introduction

From the 18th-century magnificence of Henry Hoar's Stourhead to the 20th-century horticultural spectacle of Lawrence Johnston's Hidcote, every National Trust garden has its own special character and unique identity. Over the decades each garden has been nurtured, developed and conserved by the hands of successive owners and gardeners and today is maintained by far fewer gardeners than was the case historically. Common to every garden, though, is the high standard of upkeep associated with National Trust gardens. The question we are often asked is 'How is it done?'

Part of the answer lies in the dedication and hard work of the National Trust's 450 gardeners and army of volunteers who together keep the Trust's 200 gardens up to standard. They may face the same problems as most gardeners, but generally on a much larger scale – some gardens cover over 162 hectacres (400 acres). Maintaining the standards expected of National Trust gardens also requires a high level of skill and knowledge and this is where the Trust's gardeners excel.

Most historic gardens, though, were not originally designed to cope with large numbers of visitors during the open season – grass paths are usually the first to suffer from heavy traffic in gardens designed for personal pleasure that now welcome over 100,000 visitors a year. And ever-increasing temperatures, storms, heavy rain and milder winters require an understanding of how to cope with the changing needs of plants and the increases in pests and disease that a shifting environment brings.

In the end, the quality of maintenance has an effect not only on day-to-day standards but also on the long-term conservation and development of gardens. What we do today can have a bearing on how the garden will look tomorrow and in decades to come, so developing our knowledge and applying the right approach or technical solution is critically important.

The National Trust is committed to passing on this extensive knowledge and skills base to the next generation of gardeners by investing in its three-year apprentice training scheme 'Careership' so that standards of conservation are maintained into the future. But there are few opportunities for visitors to pick up these traditional skills, which in many cases have been handed down from gardener to gardener.

This book aims to bridge that gap, by sharing the collective wisdom of our Head Gardeners' particular areas of expertise, which are often specific to the gardens they care for. Many of the techniques described in this book can be applied to small domestic gardens and, hopefully, the book will also give an insight into how each of our gardens is run and how particular features such as glass houses or kitchen gardens are maintained.

I am immensely proud of the generosity and effort that all the gardeners who work for the National Trust have put into this book. May it be a testament in years to come of their skills and deep commitment to the historic gardens in their expert care.

Mike Calnan
Head of Gardens and Parks, 2008

Planting and Maintenance

Ferns

Ferns are probably one of the groups of plants we take for granted in the garden or the house but can often be the ideal plant for that 'problem place'.

Hardy ferns

Ferns can be used effectively in a group to 'soften' planting or used singly as specimens to add a dramatic architectural dimension to parts of the garden. The other advantage of hardy ferns in the outdoors is that they will tolerate conditions that many other plants would find unacceptable, for example under trees, north-facing aspects or in wet areas of gardens.

I like to use evergreen ferns that do not die down in winter but continue to look 'lush' even in the harshest temperatures. Plants such as the shaggy shield fern (*Polystichum aculeatum*), hard shield fern (*Dryopteris cycadina*) or holly fern (*Cyrtomium falcatum* 'Rochfordianum') look good all year round.

As far as soil conditions are concerned, it has to be said that there are fern species to suit every type of soil. There are some ferns hardy to us at Tatton Park, which despite the fact that they die down in winter are definitely worth having in a

Sam Youd,
Garden Manager
TATTON PARK,
CHESHIRE

The 24-hectare (60-acre) garden at Tatton Park has been planted by four generations of the Egerton family from the mid 1700s. Apart from the stunning spring rhododendron display, other spectacular features include a large Fernery with a collection of tree ferns, a Japanese Garden, fully restored Kitchen Garden and Orchard, complete with Pineapple House.

garden, especially near the pond. One of my favourites is Japanese royal fern (*Osmunda regalis*). This plant produces wonderful curled-up fronds in the spring, which eventually unfurl like a snake, to stunning effect. Eventually the fern can grow anything up to 2m (6½ft) high and, once established, it is almost impossible to kill. As autumn approaches, the leaf colour changes to a rich golden brown, giving some great effects across the garden as it reflects the late afternoon sun.

The roots of the plants, which are very tough, were often dug up and mixed with sphagnum moss to provide compost for orchids. Propagation of *Osmunda* is by single division but beware, it has extremely strong roots so it is often best to 'chop' it into two rather than struggle any other way.

Ferns inside

The Victorians were the ones who probably made the best use of ferns inside. Low light levels in houses of the era and somewhat damp conditions were ideal for certain ferns.

Maidenhair ferns (*Adiantum*) are a group of ferns that spring to mind for such tough conditions. Maidenhair fern (*Adiantum raddianum*) is the most popular species from which many amazing cultivars have been bred. They enjoy a minimum temperature of around 10°C (50°F) with a fairly high humidity, making them an ideal subject for bathrooms. These ferns produce really 'frothy' foliage, which works well mixed with other pot plants.

There are other interesting ferns that will survive at cooler temperatures but are not hardy outside. Japanese carrot fern (*Onychium japonicum*) is so called as the fine fronds resemble carrot-like foliage. It grows to about 60cm (2ft). European chain fern (*Woodwardia radicans*) is another good cold-house fern, which is very dramatic. It is a big, strong growing plant with dramatic fronds up to 2m (6½ft) in length. The foliage is very open but the stems gracefully arch down to the floor. In their natural habitat, the young plants that are produced on the ends of these arching 'fronds' touch the ground, take root and start to grow.

Tree ferns

In recent years, there has been an increasing trend for growing tree ferns outside, no doubt spurred on by talk of climate change. However, tree ferns that are natives of Australia and New Zealand should be obtained from sustainable sources and need careful attention through the winter. If you are growing them in containers then they obviously can be used outside and brought in for winter, so that makes life easier.

If you are growing plants such as *Dicksonia* outside in a permanent position, there are a few things to remember. First, the roots of tree ferns tend to be on the outside of the stem so they need to be kept moist. Secondly, as a result of the above, the plants do not have any actual roots and this makes them quite unstable. Thirdly, they are not totally hardy in severe conditions.

Care then has to be taken to plant *Dicksonia* outside in a sheltered position. In winter they will need the 'crowns' of the plants wrapping to protect them from excess cold or excess moisture collecting in the crowns, which might freeze. The trick, of course, is to take off the cover at the correct time in spring so as not to inhibit the new growth or cause rotting in the crown.

Tips

- Ferns love moisture.
- Ferns dislike strong sunlight.
- Ferns love growing in ground enriched with organic material.

Small trees for small gardens

Types of trees

Although there is a wide choice of garden trees, there are far fewer small trees available for use where space is a premium. Suitable small garden trees fall into three groups.

The first group contains clear-stemmed trees that are naturally small or slow growing, or have a distinct habit that limits their size. These include the Japanese maples (*Acer palmatum*), the flowering dogwoods (*Cornus florida* and *C. kousa*) and the weeping silver pear (*Pyrus salicifolia* 'Pendula'), or the traditional conical or pyramidal shape of the garden conifers, such as *Chamaecyparis pisifera* 'Filifera Aurea'.

The second group includes large tree-like shrubs that are commonly grown as small garden trees and are often grown with multi-stemmed trunks that originate from ground level. In many cases regular pruning is required to maintain these clear stems. This group includes the serviceberry (*Amelanchier lamarckii*), Chinese privet (*Ligustrum lucidum*) or the Chilean fire bush (*Embothrium coccineum*).

The remaining group contains trees that respond to regular annual or biennial pruning and due to this pollarding treatment can be kept

Mike Buffin,
Gardens and Parks
Advisor (Southern)
HEELIS, NATIONAL
TRUST CENTRAL
OFFICE, SWINDON,
WILTSHIRE

Trees bring great beauty into our gardens as they herald the changing seasons and grace our lives with a stunning array of attributes. Selecting a tree for smaller spaces is one of the most challenging decisions that any gardener will face.

smaller. The following trees respond well to this treatment: Indian bean tree (*Catalpa bignonioides* 'Aurea'); the silver wattle or mimosa (*Acacia dealbata*) or the small-leaved lime (*Tilia cordata* 'Winter Orange').

The many benefits of planting trees

The visual beauty of a tree is often the main reason why it is planted, and in many cases such a selection will be based on the showiness of its flowers, foliage, fruit, bark or twigs, or even its shape or habit. Trees are also planted to create a focal point, to provide shade or create a microclimate to protect other plants, to screen, to hide or focus on a garden feature, or even to enhance a design feature. For example, a tight conical tree such as Rocky Mountain juniper (*Juniperus scopulorum* 'Skyrocket') can be used to great effect to enhance a Mediterranean design.

However, garden trees can also bring many other benefits into the garden, and these may include:

- The shade cast by a tree can help to reduce the temperature in the shade during summer and help to keep the immediate area a few degrees cooler.
- Trees hold pollutants on their leaves, which fall harmlessly when the leaves are shed and the pollutants are absorbed into the soil. As the leaves are broken down they recycle their nutrients back into the soil.
- Tree roots bind the soil together and can help limit the effects of soil erosion, a common problem during rainstorms.
- Trees can filter and slow the wind and thus prevent damage to other garden plants.
- Trees provide habitat and shelter for a vast array of garden inhabitants.

In a garden space for trees is always a limiting factor and will govern the size and numbers that can be planted.

Where and how

Although the selection of a garden tree may seem fairly straightforward, a
number of issues may affect the way that the tree will grow in the garden,
so it is essential to understand the nature and make-up of the site before
selecting your tree. To achieve this, consider the following:

- What is the type and make-up of the garden soil? You will need to record
  and understand your soil pH and soil type.
- How will local climate and weather affect the tree's growth and survival?
- For what purpose is the tree being planted? Is it to add a sense of scale, to
  screen unsightly buildings, to create shade for other plants, to add beauty,
  or for wildlife or shelter?
- How much space is available to plant your tree and allow it to mature?
- Will the tree have seasonal colour, or is it required to provide a foil for
  other plants, in which case might an evergreen tree be more suitable?

Tip

Selecting a tree that performs through a number of seasons is important
in a garden. For example, the Chinese paper bark maple, *Acer griseum*,
has cinnamon-coloured bark that flakes, followed by fiery autumn
colour and attractive seeds, so it will grace a garden throughout the
different seasons. Trees are very long-lived compared to other garden
plants, and their selection, positioning and aftercare requires careful
consideration, since established trees can be very difficult to relocate.

Using semi-tender plants

With recent mild winters, we have found it interesting to experiment with those plants whose hardiness lies on the boundaries of current winter temperatures. Increasingly, plants once considered too tender to make it through the winter, survive and flourish. Many of these semi-tender plants have strong architectural presence, providing important structure to Packwood's distinctive style of planting. Vivid flower colour and extended season of interest are also often attributes, with some flowering up to the first frosts and beyond. At Packwood a semi-tender plant is one that can withstand temperatures between 0°C (32°F) and -5°C (23°F), over-wintering in the ground with little or no protection.

Various factors influence a semi-tender plant's chances of surviving the winter; temperature alone is not always decisive. Exposure to cold, drying winds or waterlogged soil can be equally devastating and a plant's age and period of establishment are important factors. Packwood does not have an unusually mild climate, but benefits from a fairly low annual rainfall of around 68cm (27in), relatively free-draining soil and, despite a sloping, exposed site, enjoys prevailing westerly winds.

Mick Evans,
Head Gardener
PACKWOOD HOUSE,
WARWICKSHIRE

The garden at Packwood is a fascinating survival of courtyards, terraces, gazebos and topiary dating back to the 16th and 17th centuries. The style of planting reflects the character of its flamboyant owner Graham Baron Ash in the 1920s and 1930s. The many walls provide protection for semi-tender plants.

Regular survivors

Plants that ten years ago were considered tender in exposed positions now regularly make it through the winter at Packwood with no protection. Plants such as *Osteospermum, Penstemon, Ceanothus, Fuchsia* and *Phygelius* are all important to our style of planting.

Exploiting micro-climates

Warm south- or west-facing walls, free draining soil and established shrubs often create micro-climates that give a degree or two of extra protection throughout the winter months. Our warm south-facing walls with their correspondingly dry soils enable us to over-winter plants such as the Australian bottlebrush (*Callistemon rigidus*), which has produced its crimson flowers for the last decade. Elsewhere Mediterranean tree mallow (*Lavatera maritima*) produces its lilac, hibiscus-like flowers until Christmas. The exotic hummingbird sage (*Salvia guaranitica*), from Brazil, commonly produces its electric blue blooms through November and December. Revelling in the same situation silverbush (*Convolvulus cneorum*), with its attractive silvery-grey leaves, has climbed a good way up the wall through a host plant. Other plants worth experimenting with in a sheltered spot include *Echium, Abutilon, Correa, Salvia* varieties and exotic geraniums.

Protecting semi-tender plants

Not all Packwood's semi-tender plants enjoy the protection of a warm wall. In exposed positions we provide winter protection in the form of wind breaks, waterproof jackets, thick mulches or improved drainage.

The showpiece of the garden is undoubtedly the Raised Terrace, with its richly coloured planting and the yew garden beyond. Despite its exposed location, several handsome semi-tender plants form the backbone of this display. Honey spurge (*Euphorbia mellifera*) from Madeira increasingly makes it through the winter months unprotected, however, during prolonged periods below -5°C (23°F) we cover the whole plant with a layer of fleece. Although these temperatures may not kill the plant they might knock it back to the ground, which would result in the loss of the early honey-scented flowers. The South African honey bush (*Melianthus major*) survives the winter under a 10-cm (4-in) mulch of compost; the large blue-green pinnate leaves look splendid as they re-grow in early summer, but to enjoy its striking chocolate-coloured flowers, it needs a more sheltered spot. Also on the terrace we provide protection to over-winter the statuesque Japanese banana (*Musa basjoo*). In November we remove the leaves, wrap the remaining stem with loft lagging and cover with plastic compost sacks, which are left in place until May. We treat tree ferns (*Dicksonia antartica*) similarly; the compost sacks protect the plants from cold, drying winds and keep the ferns moist. At the foot of the north-facing terrace wall we grow the Taiwanese rice paper plant (*Tetrapanax papyrifer*), which makes a grand statement with its giant palmate leaves. They seem to enjoy this situation, but as a precaution we protect them with a net screen from December to March.

Plants such as succulents stand a far greater chance of surviving the winter if their roots are kept dry. Flanking the terrace steps are stone pots containing *Agave americana*, the steely-blue succulent. These are rooted in pure gravel for swift drainage and are covered in November with fine nylon netting to protect them from icy winds.

Tips

- The larger the specimen you plant the greater the chance of its survival. As the plant matures it can withstand lower temperatures and minor changes in soil condition.
- Never prune semi-tender perennials in autumn or winter unless unavoidable, in which case protect the plant with either a thick mulch or fine nylon netting.
- Always experiment – it's the best way to learn.

Plants in containers

Some basic rules for successful container growing

No matter what the type of container, whether a grand lead planter or a simple planted teapot, all need to provide plants with the right balance of conditions for good growth, and essential to this is the compost used. The basic rules are as follows:

Air: roots need oxygen to grow so good drainage is essential; coarse gravel is fine or I use. bark chips. With poor drainage the plant can become waterlogged and roots die. Too much drainage and the compost will drain too rapidly so water is wasted, and with it the nutrients.

Light: most container subjects prefer full sun for much of the day to promote good flowering. There are occasions when ferns and leafy subjects can be used to good effect in a shady spot; try *Impatiens, Nicotiana* and *Convolvulus sabatius.*

Water: generally the best containers are sumptuous with foliage and flower, and need constant attention on an almost daily basis as they progress into late season. Water loss is going to increase in a breezy open site, so aim for a

Peter Hall,
Head Gardener
POWIS CASTLE,
POWYS, WALES

Powis Castle combines architectural splendour with bold and varied planting that has evolved over 400 years with among the finest 17th-century Italianate terracing remaining in Britain. More than 30 large pots are planted annually at Powis to provide continual displays of colour and form through summer and autumn, embellishing the terraces and enhancing the richly planted borders.

sheltered location. Automated drip watering is effective in minimizing water wastage as well as saving time, but generally the best effect is achieved by close attention. Planted containers really have to be a labour of love.

Nutrients: the potting compost used at Powis is a peat-free compost mix combining ground bark, composted woodchip and sterilized loam – similar to a John Innes type mix but with more organic matter. The importance of obtaining the best-quality compost cannot be over stressed, as it provides the essential foundation for the roots with the proper air space and drainage ability, as well as holding on to nutrients and gradually releasing them as the plants develop. I add slow-release fertilizer to the garden containers to provide a longer-term feed, and supplement this later with liquid feeding, usually about six weeks after placing out.

Choosing a plant

The range of plants that can be used in containers is almost as limitless as the opportunities to experiment and show off your prowess at growing and combining plants. Many of the most dramatic containers at Powis are for summer-long display and must provide continuous interest for at least four months. Planting is done from mid April in the nursery so that by late May they are filled enough to be placed in the garden. A good idea is to have a central feature plant upon which you can build and expand the design, for example *Fuchsia triphylla* cultivars are excellent both for rich foliage and flower, as are the old, scented pelargoniums such as 'Clorinda' or 'Scarlet Pet'. Favourite trailing plants include the superb double red nasturtium 'Hermine Grashof' with its round leaves, or *Lobelia richardsonii* of clearest blue, or the soft yellow flower and bronze stems of *Oxalis vulcanicola* – all provide long and durable flowering.

Choosing a pot

Provided the cultural needs of the plant are supplied, any container can be used. There are, however, a couple of important points to consider, and one that is sometimes overlooked is how to get the plant out of the pot at the end of the year. Traditional pots are slightly wider at the top than the bottom so the contents can be easily removed without damaging plant or pot.

The second point is that cheap clay pots tend to be fired at lower temperatures, hence they are cheaper to make, but the pot will absorb more water than a more expensive pot fired at a high temperature. When it freezes the expanding ice crystals within the clay fracture the pot, so if leaving them out over the winter it makes good sense to insulate the sides to prevent freezing. Alternatively, bring them indoors in cold spells, or buy good-quality high-temperature fired pots that are frost proof.

Tip

It is commonly thought that extra feed will make extra-fast growth, but over feeding can result in the opposite. When soil water becomes too rich in nutrients, water is actually drawn out of the plant cells by a process called exosmosis, which causes the plant to wilt as though it were dry. Do please follow closely the instructions when applying feed.

Summer bedding

Summer bedding can be the crowning glory of any garden. The intensity of the colours, the longevity of the flowers and the sheer diversity of the plant range means there is always something new to try. As with all things there are good practices and bad practices when picking a bedding scheme, but there are a few simple rules to follow as outlined below.

Choosing bedding plants

When looking for a bedding plant there are several things I take into account. Colour is important, together with the ultimate height and spread of the plant, the longevity of its flowering season, its ability to cope with ever hotter, drier summers and, perhaps the most important and often overlooked, a good healthy plant to start with.

Putting your schemes together

People often talk about shape and form when they are looking at plants, but bedding is less about shape, form and permanence than colour, lashings of colour, put together in a way that is pleasing on the eye. For this I find a colour wheel invaluable.

Paul Farnell,
Head Gardener
WADDESDON
MANOR,
BUCKINGHAMSHIRE

Waddesdon Manor is renowned for its seasonal bedding displays. The Parterre alone can use up to 200,000 bedding plants annually. The beds are raised up in the high Victorian style to create maximum impact from the bedding displays.

There are four ways of describing colour schemes:

- **monochromatic:** using a single colour in its various hues and tints
- **analogous (related):** this is when colours are used that are neighbours on the colour wheel
- **contrasting:** colours that are directly opposite each other on the colour wheel
- **polychromatic (rainbow):** when colours from all parts of the wheel are used

Discounting the polychromatic scheme, there are three ways of putting these colours together in a harmonious way, the most subtle of which is to use tints and shades of a single colour. The most restful way is to match colours that lie next to each other on the colour wheel, while the boldest is to use contrasting colours, which are opposite on the colour wheel. However, it is important to remember that you are not dealing with a block of colour as you would when painting a wall, for example, as you always have the various shades of green that make up the background of the plant showing through and the flowers often have a different colour eye, perhaps starting off with a very intense colour that then fades as they age. All these factors need to be considered when designing a bedding display.

Planning bedding schemes on the scale of those at Waddesdon is a challenging and time-consuming practice. I am usually planning the next bedding scheme a full 12 months before it is required but all my efforts are worthwhile when a scheme comes together and sits comfortably on the eye.

Care of bedding plants

Bedding plants are usually quite robust, but having said this, at Waddesdon Manor we are growing them in the same beds year after year, so here are some of my tips to keep your plants looking good. Firstly, it is important to have a good, healthy plant to start with. Soil is the next consideration. Soil science has come a long way over the past few years, confirming what our forefathers knew – that adding well-rotted organic material to the soil improved the quality of the plant. We now know that it is due in part to micro-organisms within the compost that are beneficial to the plant, so good soil preparation is essential. Most bedding plants are annuals and their sole purpose is to flower and set seed to continue their species. Regular dead heading of the plants will prolong the flowering of your bedding, and while doing this you are close up to the plant so you can tell if there are any problems with pests or diseases that may be present.

Feeding

Some bedding plants can be quite heavy feeders. I use an organic seaweed-based fertilizer at the start of the season and during August I supplementary feed with an organic liquid fertilizer every two weeks or so. If you are using liquid feed I suggest that you use it at half the recommended strength; your plants will flower just as well and be tougher and more disease resistant.

Tips

- Regular dead heading will prolong the flowering season of your plants.
- Check regularly for pests and diseases.
- Pinch out foliage bedding plants regularly to encourage more foliage.

Topiary

Topiary, usually evergreen, can provide structure and a sense of geometry and balance to a garden in a very formal way. However, it also allows full rein to human eccentricity and can be puzzling and humorous, even bizarre. It's also an excellent example of 'slow gardening'.

A brief history

Topiary as a garden art form has a long history and happily is back in fashion again. In Ancient Rome actual gardening work was done by slaves and it was the *topiarius* who looked after the ornamental garden or *topia*. Clipped hedging became hugely popular in Renaissance Italy and by the late Middle Ages in Britain a formal style had developed using hedges in elaborate, geometric patterns, mazes and labyrinths and shaped forms grown as standards.

The 17th century is seen as the golden age when topiary became an essential part of the formal landscape, culminating in the giddy excess of Versailles in France, whose style spread across the great gardens of Europe.

Having been swept away by the landscape movement, only to be revived by the Victorians, topiary continued to thrive into the 20th century

Phil Rollinson,
Head Gardener
MOUNT STEWART,
COUNTY DOWN,
NORTHERN
IRELAND

Situated close to the shores of Strangford Lough on the Ards Peninsula, this 36-hectare (90-acre) garden houses a wonderfully diverse and exotic plant collection from around the world. Topiary features prominently in several of the formal garden rooms, which lie close to the mansion house.

as part of the Arts and Crafts style, as at Hidcote Manor in Gloucestershire and here at Mount Stewart where Edith, Lady Londonderry, created the formal gardens in the 1920s and 1930s.

Our parterres are hedged with an unusual choice of species such as heather, berberis, hebe and bay laurel. Huge arches of leyland cypress and large domed bay trees provide a strong Mediterranean, architectural structure. The Shamrock Garden is enclosed by a yew hedge with the top topiarized to depict a humorous family hunting scene adapted from the Psalter of Queen Mary Tudor. Other iconic images include the Irish harp with two British crowns in the background.

Choosing the right plant

The most common plants for topiary are yew and box because of their small leaves and dense growth, and their ability to regenerate readily, not only from clipping, but from hard pruning, if necessary. Lady Londonderry hated box, therefore you won't find it anywhere in the garden at Mount Stewart. But other evergreens do just as well, such as holly, privet, Portuguese laurel and even ivy. You could try deciduous plants, too, for example beech, hawthorn and hornbeam.

Why not experiment with more unusual subjects? Try Chinese holly (*Osmanthus delavayi*), mock privet (*Phillyrea*), *Escallonia* and *Euonymus*. Or, for milder locations like ours, try bottlebrushes (*Callistemon*). We have six grown as standards, which make great lollipops.

Creating your chosen shape

Simple shapes can be cut freehand but the more complex the design the greater the need for a guiding framework. These are readily available to buy or you can make your own using a variety of materials, such as fencing wire, chicken wire, rods, stakes and bamboo canes. The framework for the hunting scene at Mount Stewart was made by a local blacksmith.

Tie in stems to the framework, pinching back any new shoots to encourage branching out and speedier covering of the frame. New growth will have to be trained to fill in gaps, tying shoots in with something that is biodegradable such as tarred string. This is best done in the growing season when the shoots are young and pliable.

Topiary doesn't have to be geometrically accurate to be of interest. Over the years they can get pretty wonky, maybe due to bad weather, pests and diseases or mistakes.

You might start with a shape in mind but end up with something totally different – go with the flow and make a feature of it.

Clipping: when and how

Ideally, once established, topiary should be clipped every four to six weeks in the growing season to retain a crisp finish. From May through to September is a good guide. Hedges need less regular attention and generally an annual trim is sufficient. Obviously, time and labour is a factor and at Mount Stewart we only have the resources for one trim per year. As our hedges and topiary are mature that's generally fine unless it's been an exceptional growing year when two trims would be better to retain the crisp, sharp outlines that are so important in a formal setting. We start trimming in June and don't finish until the end of September. Always be wary of late or early frosts, which can scorch new growth badly or even kill plants, especially box. Because of our coastal location, salt scorch can be a problem, leaving unsightly, damaged foliage, which may need to be cut back.

Topiary takes up your time and patience and lots of standing back and looking. For intricate specimens you should use scissors, secateurs and hand shears. Electric hedge trimmers are good for less intricate work and for hedges. Try to avoid petrol-driven trimmers – they are noisy, smelly and generally heavy to use.

Safety

Don't forget you are using sharp cutting implements. Always wear proper personal protective equipment and watch out for those cables when using electric trimmers. Keep the blades well clear of the cables – residual circuit breakers are a must. Make sure ladders and steps are firmly secure. Here, at Mount Stewart hedge trimming can be a great spectator sport; our visitors are always curious but you must always concentrate.

Routine care

Just as for any freestanding shrubs, weeding, watering and mulching are essential to promote healthy, vigorous growth. Feeding during the growing season with a good, balanced fertilizer, twice if possible, is good practice, particularly if any renovation pruning has to be done. This may be necessary if hedges or topiary have been neglected and have grown badly out of shape. Yew and box are both excellent at regenerating from severe pruning, right back to the trunk if necessary.

We find rabbits are partial to doing their own trimming on young yews and most other things for that matter!

We rarely get snow here but for those who are still unaffected by climate change, snowfall on topiary can be very damaging because of the extra weight on branches. Gently knock it off any flat surfaces or better still use netting over your topiary pieces to alleviate the problem.

Tips

- Smaller plants are best when creating new hedges or specimens – they acclimatize to local conditions much more quickly than larger plants.
- If possible, clip little and often to retain that crisp finish.
- Always use sharp tools and ones you are familiar with.
- Take time to stand back and look – frequently and from a number of viewpoints.
- Have fun!

Staking herbaceous perennials

How and when to stake

Usually we use about 60 bundles of pea sticks, each bundle containing about 30 sticks all around 2.5m (8ft) long. We prefer the twiggy pea sticks as when the plants have grown to their full height they are less conspicuous and offer more support than straight hazel sticks. The staking of the garden is dependent on the season and is done on an as-needed basis but generally plants are staked about the end of April, beginning of May or when the plants are about 30–45cm (1–1½ft) tall.

Traditional herbaceous borders are generally graded according to their height so we have about four different sizes of pea sticks ranging from stakes for the shorter, middle and tall groups of plants, to very tall sticks for exceptionally large specimens that are tied on individually. These are usually at the back of the border, upright plants that are surrounded by other tall herbaceous perennials or a wall of yew hedge, which helps to distract from the sort of drumstick effect you get when bulky plants are tied to a single stake.

The general idea is to trim the pea stick to within two-thirds of the final height of the plant and to use sufficient sticks, usually placed around the edge of the clump, to provide support without

Paul Underwood,
Head Gardener
BLICKLING HALL,
NORFOLK

The Norfolk climate is not a gentle one and winds can batter or flatten even the most upstanding plants. At Blickling, staking on the parterre is therefore essential and is also traditional. From late winter the forester on the Blickling Estate cuts the hazel pea sticks from Blickling's woods. These are cut early before the hazel comes into leaf and stored in the sheds in the garden so that during wet weather an early start can be made by cutting them to size.

interfering with the habit of the plant. These need to be pushed well into the ground but care needs to be taken not to damage the roots – one of the most common problems with staking is that the stake is not pushed far enough into the ground. For plants that need support close to the flowers, twiggy hazel can be bent over at the right angle to form an effective cage, and if this is done early enough then it can be hidden by the foliage of the plant and can protect the plant against even the worst weather.

Of course, there are many ways to stake herbaceous borders but I think hazel pea sticks make one of the best and least obtrusive methods when used correctly, at the right time. Other ways include using other pea sticks, such as birch, or using proprietary or homemade devices such as link-ring stakes or wire-mesh rings – where the stems grow through the support and eventually hide it. Single or groups of canes can also be used or you can even use black plastic wide-mesh netting – this method is only really useful for large borders filled only with herbaceous perennials but if placed over the whole border, except for the very front, it can support the plants without making them appear too stiff.

You may wish to tie your plant to a support as in the case of delphiniums and other tall, mostly single-stemmed perennials where string or twine is tied in a figure of eight at various heights as it grows. You may also wish to use metal stakes as we do with Scotch thistle (*Onopordum*), although care should be taken so that the string does not cut into the plant.

Whether to stake at all

Of course, after considering all this, you must decide whether the time and effort of staking and tying is necessary at all. Some people would actually prefer to see the natural habit of the plant or even to let it lean or flop, rather than see it restrained by stakes that don't necessarily look attractive and require a lot of time and effort to use. But even those who don't want to do any staking must admit that the damage done to certain plants, especially if they are tall and fragile, weak stemmed, grown in exposed windy sites or grown up by a tall building, can be devastating and it is to these people that I can recommend using twiggy hazel sticks.

Tips

- In all cases do not leave staking until after the plant has collapsed.
- Make sure that you push the stake well into the ground and if the ground is particularly hard, pick a day after it has rained.
- At the end of season, store the stakes for reuse, or if they are past their best hazel pea sticks can easily be chipped and used as an attracive and practical woodland mulch.

The conservatory all year round

Today conservatories are popular again and are a feature of many homes, with many different uses, from a place to relax when the weather is not suitable to sit outside, to an extra room possibly for dining in or as a playroom for the children. Plants can be added to brighten up the room, however it is used, with as many or few plants as you like. Plus, for the keen gardener, there is an opportunity to grow an exciting wide range of tender plants to fill the room, possibly dedicating it to the cultivation of one type, such as orchids, all year round or citrus plants for part of the year, as at Hanbury.

Aspect

The direction that the conservatory faces will affect the choice of plants. For example, if it faces north and is shaded most of the day the range of plants will be vastly different to those suitable for a south-facing position. Few of us are able to decide the position of a conservatory, as its position is normally dictated by the available space to build it. A south-facing aspect means that the conservatory will be warm on a sunny day in winter but extremely hot on a summer's day. If it

Neil Cook,
Head Gardener
HANBURY HALL,
WORCESTERSHIRE

The early 18th-century garden at Hanbury Hall designed by George London was re-created between 1993 and 1994 by the National Trust. Beyond this garden away from the Hall is the mid 18th-century Orangery. This is now used as it was originally intended, to over-winter a wonderful collection of citrus plants.

were possible to choose, an east- or west-facing conservatory would give the widest range of plants to grow there.

Heating

The amount and type of heating in your conservatory will be a deciding factor for what types of plants can be grown. Keeping the conservatory frost free with a minimum temperature of 5–7°C (41–44.5°F) would be the cheapest option and allow a good range of plants to be grown. The next temperature would be 10°C (50°F) minimum, which is more suited to a wider range of plants. If the conservatory is part of the house, keeping it at 15–21°C (59–70°F) would be comfortable for both plants and human beings, but care must be taken to avoid a drastic drop in temperature at night when the central heating is switched off.

Humidity

Humidity is linked to heating, as the artificial heat that is used in the home greatly reduces humidity. This lack of humidity is one of the possible reasons citrus plants lose leaves when brought inside for winter protection. If orchids are to be grown successfully they need high humidity as temperatures rise, but if you have furnishings in your conservatory that might be damaged by a humid atmosphere then succulents and cacti would be a better choice.

Ventilation

The question of adequate ventilation in a conservatory for plants is often not considered as carefully as it should be; there should be provision for airflow to keep the room cool when the sun is shining on the conservatory. This is a particularly important issue to consider when the house is empty, without compromising the security of the rest of the house.

Pests

The protected environment of a conservatory provides the ideal conditions for pests to thrive, but is also well suited for the use of biological control to help combat them. This means using one insect to control another insect that is a pest. Specific predators are needed to control each type of pest. If aphids are found, wipe them off or spray them with insecticidal soap. See pages 105–108 for advice on environmentally friendly pest and disease control.

Plants

Taking all the above into consideration, here are a few options and types of plants to grow. These are only suggestions, as the list of possible plants is vast.

* **Unheated, but not south-facing unless used only to over-winter:** plants like the bottlebrush (*Callistemon*), mimosa (*Acacia dealbata*), oleander (*Nerium*) and the climbing rose *Rosa banksii* could be grown.
* **Minimum 5°C (41°F):** Bougainvillea, citrus, plumbago and bird of paradise flower (*Strelitzia*) are good choices.
* **Above 12°C (53.5°F):** exotics such as papyrus (*Cyprus*), *Heliconia* and *Philodendron* for the jungle effect can be grown.

Specialist plants, such as orchids, can be grown just as they would in the house. There is a range that will grow in temperatures of 10–24°C (50–75°F), including *Cymbidium, Dendrobium* and *Oncidium*. If they are to be kept in the conservatory throughout the year attention should be paid as much to the maximum temperature as to the minimum.

Tips

- If you have a few plants that need higher humidity, stand each pot on a saucer containing gravel and fill with water, being careful not to allow the base of the plant to touch the water.
- Children are fascinated by cacti despite the prickles and they can be a great way to get them interested in plants.

Planting for winter interest

Colour in winter

Producing colour without using lots of flowers makes winter gardening both challenging and exciting. Colour can be found in various plant parts. Coloured stems such as dogwoods (*Cornus*), willow (*Salix*) and brambles (*Rubus*) give permanent colour for at least six months of the year even on the greyest of days. The bold leaf colour of oleaster (*Elaeagnus*) and Mexican orange (*Choisya*) (both green and yellow types) will assist in making excellent backgrounds to show off other plants.

Trees having good bark interest such as birch (*Betula*), acers and some *Prunus* varieties give both visual and good tactile qualities.

Berries and fruits add interest although some are eaten earlier than others. Types we try are holly, cotoneaster, beauty berry (*Callicarpa*), apple (*Malus*) and the unusual strawberry tree (*Arbutus*).

Careful choices of ground-cover plants are important as you will need to have colours that can complement the surrounding plants such as *Euonymus* 'Emerald Gaiety' with *Viburnum bodnantense* 'Dawn' or colours to give a strong contrast such as *Luzula sylvatica* 'Aurea' with *Mahonia aquifolium* 'Apollo'.

Richard Todd,
Head Gardener
ANGLESEY ABBEY
GARDEN, LODE,
CAMBRIDGESHIRE

In 1926 Lord Fairhaven of Anglesey Abbey began to create a 40-hectare (98-acre) garden on the edge of Cambridgeshire's Fenland, continuing until his death in 1966. A beautiful commemorative Winter Garden was opened in 1998 and by following the serpentine path you are led through a spectacular variety of colours and scents.

Good-sized bold groupings are important for impact as single plants will get lost in the general mix.

Activating all the senses is what winter gardening is all about and the sense of smell is a must to be explored. There is a vast choice of shrubs that can be used, including *Mahonia, Viburnum,* honeysuckle (*Lonicera*), wintersweet (*Chimonanthus*) and Christmas box (*Sarcococca*) to name a few. We often position these on corners to give pleasant surprises, especially on days that are still and warmer. Using the protection of nearby trees can help to prevent frost damage.

Being aware of the sun's direction is the key for showing off some interesting features for plants that have good branch formation such as corkscrew hazel (*Corylus avellana* 'Contorta') or plants with attractive thorns or flaking bark. Remember the winter sun is low and will shine through things rather than directly from above.

We use dark foliage backgrounds to lift plants into view as well as the use of the dark layer of leaf mould under plants like dogwoods and brambles.

Take advantage of planting spring bulbs under deciduous shrubs so that a good display is enjoyed before new foliage blocks out the light. Taller flowering bulbs can be added to ground-cover areas, for example the use of narcissus with ivy and crocus with *Vinca minor*.

Snowdrops and spring bulbs

Anglesey Abbey's collection of snowdrops is approaching 200 in number and continues to bring interest and pleasure, especially by noting the many differences between varieties. There are varieties flowering from October onwards but it is January that really heralds the arrival of this fascinating flower of the woodland or woodland edge.

Snowdrops will grow in reasonably exposed sites but often prefer dappled light. Growing them in thick, lush grass areas is not advised as the grass will dominate and stifle future development.

There are a host of varieties for the more serious collector to choose from, but for most it would probably either be the common *Galanthus nivalis* or its double form 'Flore Pleno' that are seen in profusion.

Clumps of bulbs can easily be divided about every five years to help increase the displays. The best time for this is just after flowering has finished and when the leaves are still green, replanting at the same depth in groups of three or four.

Other bulbs that can equally give great displays in similar conditions would include the following: winter aconite (*Eranthis*), flowering at the same time as snowdrops; *Scilla* and *Chionodoxa*, which are excellent at seeding and spreading under tree canopies; crocus species like *tommasinianus*, which will readily seed and spread; *Anemone blanda*; and finally dog's tooth violet (*Erythronium*) that loves to grow in dappled sunlight in woodland.

Tips

- Regular pruning of coloured stems is essential as the best colour is always on the current year's growth; prune in late March.
- Use the low winter sun to either highlight or backlight plants for best effect.
- Strong contrasting colours or shapes will speak loudly and draw immediate attention.
- Aim to experiment with combining bulbs and other plants such as snowdrops with early miniature iris and hellebore, or using the foliage of *Cyclamen hederifolium* or bergenia as a background.

Planting and establishing trees

Trees make a huge impact on the landscape around us. They provide shade in the summer, and a valuable habitat for many insects, birds and mammals. There is evidence to show that being around trees and plants can improve your mood, reduce your blood pressure and enhance your overall well-being.

Choosing the tree

Smaller trees, known as whips, which are a year old and usually around 40–60cm (15½–23½in) in height, establish best and require less immediate aftercare, such as watering; however, if it is instant impact that is required, a larger (and more expensive) specimen may be chosen, but beware as the chances of success are diminished with the greater size, and the amount of care required will increase until the tree is established.

Preparing the ground

Planting is best done when trees are dormant between November and March, well before the stresses of the hotter and drier summer months. When planting a whip, make a simple slot in the ground, deep enough to accommodate the whole of the tap root. If planting a larger tree with a

Katherine Alker, Gardener-in-Charge
CROOME PARK, WORCESTERSHIRE

Croome Park was Lancelot 'Capability' Brown's first complete landscape. The parkland, shrubberies and lakeside gardens are being restored to their former glory using original plans and plant bills. Extensive tree planting has been undertaken in the parkland with species such as oak, beech, plane and lime.

root ball, dig a hole slightly wider than the root ball itself. Be careful not to dig too deep a hole as this could create a sump, which could easily become waterlogged. However, ensure that the base and sides of the hole have been 'roughened up' so that the roots are able to penetrate the surrounding soil.

Planting the tree

Phew – after all that digging you're now ready to plant your tree. Sometimes a tree will have outgrown its pot, and its roots may even protrude through the bottom of the container. Don't be afraid to reach for your secateurs and prune the offending roots back in order to free the tree from the pot. Constrained roots need to be teased away from the main root ball so that they can readily grow out into the ground. It is also important that the tree is not planted too deeply as this could cause the base of the trunk to rot. Be aware that nurseries sometimes top their pots up with too much compost: if this is the case, remove the excess to expose the original soil level (a change in bark colour may help you identify this).

Getting the best from your tree

At Croome Park, we have added mycorrhizal fungi to the soil when tree planting. The term 'mycorrhiza' comes from the Greek words for fungus (*myco*) and root (*rhiza*), and refers to the cooperative relationship between the two, essential for the tree's health. These fungi are vital in root development; aid water uptake and also improve soil structure by either separating clay particles, or clumping together sand particles. If you have trouble finding mycorrhizal products at your local garden centre, try a specialist tree nursery or use the internet, if necessary.

In addition to using our fungal friends, it is good practice to 'top dress' newly planted trees with a good general-purpose plant food; at Croome we like to use organic bone meal. There is some advantage to leaving this task until the springtime since the nitrogen element of the fertilizer can be leached out of the ground by heavy winter rain.

Tree protection

Protecting the trees from deer, rabbits and squirrels has been essential at Croome Park. We have used 1.5-m (5-ft) tall plastic guards with a strong stake to keep our deer at bay. A secondary benefit of the guards is that they create a beneficial microclimate in which the tree can grow, both retaining moisture and sheltering the tree from wind and frost.

We have used a mulch mat made of natural, renewable hemp fibres around each tree in order to suppress weed growth without the need for chemical spraying. Although this might seem to be an inessential extra cost, the mats last for several years, giving enough time for your tree to establish without competition from weeds.

Tips

- For successful planting and establishment of trees, choose young,
  healthy specimens appropriate for your soil type. Talk to an expert,
  your local nursery or garden centre if you're not sure what to buy.
- Use mycorrhizal planting products to encourage root growth and
  good tree health.
- Feed with bone meal or another general-purpose fertilizer. Look for
  one with plenty of 'trace' elements in addition to nitrogen,
  potassium, phosphorus (N. P. K).
- Protect from the elements and local wildlife as necessary with an
  appropriate tree guard.
- And remember … timing is everything. Only plant your tree in the
  winter months: if you've not bought your tree by Easter, hang up
  your spade until Halloween!

Pruning roses

There are no secrets to successful pruning: sharp secateurs, strong gloves and an understanding of 'why' as well as 'when' and 'how' are all that you require.

When?

Early March is an excellent time to prune repeat-flowering roses such as hybrid teas (large flowered), floribundas (cluster flowered) and most modern shrub and climbing varieties. For comfort's sake, choose a mild, dry day if possible, simply to make the work more enjoyable.

Why?

Roses will survive with the minimum of attention, but if they are to thrive a certain amount of careful pruning should be undertaken. The aim of pruning is to:
* develop shape
* control size
* maintain vigour
* encourage flowering
* provide a happy and healthy plant

A well-shaped rose bush is an adornment to any garden, even in March. Maintain a balanced and open-branched structure by pruning main stems

David Stone,
Head Gardener
MOTTISFONT
ABBEY, NEAR
ROMSEY,
HAMPSHIRE

Set in the heart of Hampshire's Test Valley, Mottisfont Abbey's 14 hectares (35 acres) of garden boasts the largest specimen of London plane tree in Britain, while the ancient walled gardens contain the National Collection of old-fashioned shrub and climbing roses.

to an outward-facing bud, and completely removing any dead or entangling stems at, or near to, ground level. Remember that a naturally tall-growing rose cannot be kept short by hard pruning. However, careful attention at the right time can help to contain strong growing varieties within manageable proportions.

How?

Most repeat-flowering roses can be divided into the following pruning groups:

Bush (hybrid tea and floribunda)

New plants should be pruned back hard to within 10–15cm (4–6in) of the ground to encourage the formation of new, strong branches from near the plant's base. In subsequent years, prune away all weak and ageing wood before reducing the remaining stems by approximately one-half to two-thirds of their length. Strong growers, such as the ever popular 'Peace' (hybrid tea) and 'Iceberg' (floribunda) can be pruned less severely. As a general rule, prune lightly for quantity of bloom, prune hard for quality of bloom.

Climbing roses

With new plants, the emphasis should be on training new shoots to cover the supporting wall or trellis. Shorter side shoots, which may have flowered the previous summer, are best pruned back to a bud or two of the main branch. As the plants develop, they may become 'leggy', with flowers held above eye level. To encourage the formation of fresh young shoots from ground level, prune away completely the occasional older stem. If such stems are stouter than 12mm (½in), you will need long-handled pruners or a small, sharp saw to cut through the stems.

Modern shrub roses

This wide and varied group of mainly repeat-flowering varieties includes the 'English' roses, such as 'Graham Thomas' and the older, but ever-popular hybrid musk varieties 'Cornelia' and 'Buff Beauty'. In general, it may not be necessary to do more than tip back the leading shoots of established plants, but I prefer to reduce all new stems by approximately one-third of their length. According to the habit of growth, some thinning out of stems may be required in order to avoid overcrowding, and hard pruning of older stems may, from time to time, prove necessary in order to encourage further new growths. Most shrub roses are best left to form largish specimens, although there are many excellent varieties available for the smaller garden.

'Old-fashioned' shrub roses

Within this large group of midsummer flowering roses, are included rambling roses such as 'Albertine', species ('wild') roses such as *Rosa moyesii* as well as the ancient *R. gallica, R.* x *damascene, R.* x *centifolia* and *R. alba*. Such roses flower best on the shoots that were produced the previous year, but will continue to bloom on older stems for several years. In general, they are best left to form naturally wide and branching shrubs, but in order to keep them within bounds, some formative pruning is beneficial. Newly planted shrubs will need little in the way of pruning for their first year or two; thereafter selected thinning of older, already flowered, stems can take place any time through July and August, when the flowering season is finished for the year. Pruning at this time will encourage the rose to produce those all-important new shoots, which will bear the best blooms in future summers. In order to maintain a robust shrub, that will 'stand on its own two feet', new shoots of the previous summer should be reduced by approximately one-third in winter, and any 'untidy' branches lightly pruned to shape.

Tips

- **March:** complete all major pruning and mulch with manure or organic (peat free) compost. Remember, prune lightly for quantity of bloom, prune hard for quality of bloom.
- **July:** remove the spent blooms from repeat-flowering varieties to encourage the development of a second crop.
- **October:** tie in new shoots of climbing roses to avoid damage by the autumn gales.
- **Any time:** enjoy your roses!

Pruning trees

Reasons for pruning

It is inevitable that trees will need pruning at some stage during their life as part of the garden. Annual inspections of the collection at Stourhead can inform us of pruning requirements within the established tree population as can routine maintenance on the younger trees. There are a number of reasons that trees might need to be pruned, as explained below.

To promote a healthy tree

When dealing with a specimen tree in a garden, remove any dead and diseased branches back to a healthy growing point. Regular inspections of young trees will highlight the need to remove branches that will potentially form tight and therefore weak forks, and will show the need to remove any crossing and rubbing branches. If these tasks are carried out when the trees are young this can prevent the need for major tree surgery in later years. In certain areas of the garden at Stourhead and with specific plants we do not remove the dead wood from the trees as this is an important habitat for many invertebrates.

Alan Power,
Head Gardener
STOURHEAD,
WILTSHIRE

Laid out in the 1740s, Stourhead is one of the most beautiful landscape gardens in Europe. The 18th-century landscape is overlaid with a remarkable collection of trees including numerous champion trees (the largest living specimen of a tree variety) and some original introductions. The trees vary in age and species and it is vital that we keep these elements within the collection.

To extend the life of a tree

Some of the practices already mentioned help to extend the life of a tree, but with certain trees, when they achieve great size and status in the garden, structural weaknesses can become apparent. In some instances it becomes necessary to reduce the weight on an individual limb by thinning out the branch network. It may be necessary to carry out an overall crown reduction; this will reduce the weight on each limb and it also reduces the wind sail capacity of the tree (the amount of pressure the wind places on the tree) and takes some pressure off the main stems.

For aesthetics

A visual inspection of a young tree will highlight any imbalances within the crown, and when caught at a young age it is easier to remove small branches that may lead to a lopsided tree, unwanted double leaders, low-growing branches and inward-growing branches.

For the garden

The framed views at Stourhead form an integral part of the overall concept in the landscape and sometimes it is necessary to remove branches that may obscure these picturesque views. It is always worth aiming to prune a tree at as young an age as possible in order to eliminate the need to leave a large pruning wound on a mature tree.

For safety

Finally, if it is seen that a limb has become potentially dangerous then its removal is essential.

When to prune

- **Autumn:** deciduous specimen trees are best pruned late in the autumn or in winter. Specimen ornamental evergreen trees can be pruned in autumn in the milder areas of the country.
- **Winter:** again, deciduous specimen trees are pruned in winter but avoid evergreen trees during the colder parts of the season.
- **Spring:** early in spring is a good time to pollard or prune back willows, conifers and broad-leafed evergreens, but avoid leaving the pruning too late in the season, when the sap will be rising.
- **Summer:** in summer when we are all busy in the garden keeping up with routine maintenance, sometimes we forget the needs of the trees, but conifers can be pruned during the summer along with broad-leafed evergreen trees.

(Note: If a tree is deemed unsafe then it may be necessary to work outside seasonal recommendations.)

Tips

- Make sure pruning tools are sharp and clean.
- Remove suckers at ground level on ornamental trees.
- Avoid heavy pruning in summer.
- Remove pruning debris as soon as possible, as this can play host to pests and diseases.
- If in doubt about when or how to prune always seek advice from an expert, such as your local tree surgeon.
- Pruning a tree forms part of your overall tree-care regime. You should also ensure the base of a young tree is free of weeds, to reduce competition for nutrients. Inspect any supports on the tree, making sure that stakes are firm and ties are not loose or too tight. Feeding a young tree with natural well-rotted leaf mulch helps it to establish, reduces competition at root level and keeps moisture in.

Lawn renovation and maintenance

'Grass is green and covers the ground, that's all you need to know' was the advice I was given many years ago as a trainee gardener. Not the best advice I have ever heard, but if you can manage the 'green' bit then you are halfway to a decent lawn.

I think that to succeed in having a good-quality lawn, you have to be prepared to spend time on some simple cultivation tasks.

Letting the soil breathe

This is important otherwise you will end up with anaerobic conditions in your lawn. To let the soil breathe you need to ensure that the build up of thatch is not excessive. This can be done by reducing the amount of clippings that are left behind after mowing, but it is still also advisable to scarify on a biannual basis. On small lawns this is best done by using a wire rake for 20 minutes at a time; if you can do more than 20 minutes then you are probably not raking vigorously enough! On large lawns it is probably best to hire a petrol-driven scarifier with a collection box, otherwise you will still have to rake up all the arising thatch. Scarifying is best done either in September or into spring, perhaps in March once

Glyn Jones,
Head Gardener
HIDCOTE MANOR
GARDEN,
GLOUCESTERSHIRE

Hidcote is situated at 180m (600ft) above sea level, in the rain shadow of the Cotswold scarp and on poor soil. But Lawrence Johnston created one of the finest gardens in England here in the early 20th century, in the Arts and Crafts style, with a superb collection of plants.

the grass is actively growing again. After scarifying you will be able to scatter seed over any bare patches.

Also, to ensure the soil remains healthy, aeration is recommended, especially on those areas that get a lot of foot traffic. Again, on small areas this is best done with a garden fork and a hired machine on large areas. After spiking, if your budget allows you can top dress with a good lawn top dressing available from garden centres; this will improve both drainage and soil condition.

As a side benefit, if you want to improve your own fitness both scarifying and aeration are excellent cardiovascular exercises if done manually.

Helping the grass grow

Once you have improved the condition of the soil, the next important thing is gently encouraging the grass to grow strongly. One of the best ways of doing this is to mow regularly, but never in the same direction for more than two or three cuts, as changing direction prevents stalky grass establishing. In spring, as mowing begins, set the mower on a higher setting, gradually lowering the height as the season progresses towards summer; for ornamental lawns never cut closer than 1.5cm (½in), but during dry periods be prepared to raise the height to 2.5cm (1in). As autumn approaches again raise the height in order to allow the grass plants to strengthen up before winter sets in. During mild winters you may need to top off the grass to prevent it becoming too long; this should be done on a high setting. Collecting the grass clippings by means of a grass box on the mower removes plant growth and nutrition, so this needs to be replaced by using fertilizers. There are some very good non-chemical ones available these days, especially those made out of poultry manures, but they do smell for a week or two after application.

If you keep your soil healthy and your grass strong this should reduce the need to control moss and weeds, as the grass will out-compete these. But after a while you may get some weed species coming into the sward and these are best knocked out with a proprietary moss or weed killer. I would avoid using the combination feed and weed type product, as it is best to either kill the weeds or feed the grass.

Tips

- Grass is one of the highest maintenance areas of the garden so if you find you don't have time for all the mowing and so on, consider creating a new border. In the long run borders require less work than grass, if well designed and planted.
- I prefer to use a rotary-type mower with a rear roller as opposed to wheels at the rear because the cut is closer and the rotary is far more durable than when using a cylinder-type mower.
- Consider planting spring bulbs in a shady corner, as these will really lift your spirits when they flower, informing you that the nicer weather is just around the corner.
- Always ensure you have enough time to relax and enjoy your garden, with a G&T to hand!

Labelling

What should be labelled?

Generally, labelling of plants is a personal preference, but should only reach a desired appropriate level. Furthermore, they should never impede or distract your attention away from the important things, namely the plants themselves. However, it is always the interesting subjects that constantly appear to have their labels missing; hopefully the next few paragraphs will help resolve some issues or stimulate ideas for labels that fit in with your garden's style.

When planning to use labels, first decide for what use the labels are intended; in most cases it will be for personal reference or visitor information, although you may wish to give more detailed information to reach a wider audience. A good starting point is to label the most important specimens or the ones whose names you don't know already or to consider those plants closest to paths, then extend to those further back in the border – but remember this is likely to encourage people to walk over the soil and plants. Don't feel that everything should be labelled; if the genus is represented in other parts of the garden only label one or two specimens.

Franklyn Tancock,
Plant Collections
Curator
HEELIS, NATIONAL
TRUST CENTRAL
OFFICE, SWINDON,
WILTSHIRE

My main role within the National Trust's central gardens and parks advisory team is to manage the central gardens and parks plant database together with all other matters relating to plant collections, including labelling. Plant labels should enhance the visitor's enjoyment and understanding, but never dominate the garden.

Which style suits my garden?

The market is flooded with various types and styles, from traditional zinc labels, which have seen great service in many gardens since Victorian times, through to environmentally friendly ones made from recycled plastic in an array of colours to suit all tastes. Your choice of font size and style should ensure the label can be read from a path or at a distance and could give the label an air of elegance while simple hand written ones will give the personal touch. I have seen security tape used to great effect in recent years, where a transparent or coloured sticky tape that uses a special printer is then positioned onto your chosen label. It has a life expectancy of about five to ten years, and is a modern version of the embossed tape that was used for many years with excellent results. When securing labels to woody plants allow for future growth, but please never tie them around the main stems or branches – too many times I've seen plants that have received years of tender loving care only to be strangled by the wire from the label.

What's in a name?

The best solution is to stick with the botanical or scientific name, which is a universal language among horticulturalists throughout the world. Although many of them can be difficult to pronounce, think how your use of botanical Latin will impress your friends and relations. Using the common name only opens the question 'What is a common name?' By their very nature, many of them vary from region to region and can cause great confusion. The only exception is for herbs and vegetables.

DIY versions

A number of National Trust properties have used ingenious ways of labelling. For example Calke Abbey in Derbyshire uses labels made from marine plywood with embossed tape, which is then given a coat of clear varnish to combat the elements. Felbrigg in Norfolk, on the other hand, uses reverse printing (white on black) onto plain paper, which is then laminated and secured to an appropriate stake. Letter punches used to stamp the names into lead labels, which then hinge onto locally made metal supports achieves the desired result at Kingston Lacy in Dorset. In the herbaceous borders of Nymans in Sussex, they continue using the traditional method of short painted stakes made from hedgerow material. Many of our kitchen gardens use hand-written white-painted wooden labels to great effect. So, never be afraid to experiment, but of course always think of the environmental impact that your solutions may have.

What is the alternative?

Are there any other options? Well, one solution is to make a simple record of your plants either in a notebook or database and ideally make a copy. The key things to record are the source, the plant name, planting date, location within the garden and any comments. A sequential number can be allocated to each plant for quick referencing. A simple plan of the bed or border using simple coordinates is another easy way of keeping track of your collection.

Tips

- Always choose a style of label that will enhance your plant collection.
- Resist turning your garden into a 'sea of labels'.
- Don't feel that everything should be labelled – if the same plant is represented in other parts of the garden you only need to label one or two specimens.
- When securing labels to plants, allow for the plant to grow – and please, never around the main stem.
- Use a reputable source for checking the spelling; don't assume that the label the plant came with will have the correct name or spelling.
- Do remember: some vermin think plant labels are sweets.

Maintenance of mixed borders

The mixed border is the main backbone of any garden and is part of what makes gardening so exciting. If planted and maintained correctly the colours of the foliage and flowers and the structure of the planting can be effective all year round.

After planting, it is very important to follow a good routine and annual programme of maintenance to get maximum benefit from the border. Even though I have a vast range of borders situated around the garden with quite different plants and shrubs in them, a very similar routine and annual maintenance programme still applies across them all. Of course, it is still a great joy to work with all the different plants in various locations.

Establishing a routine

Your routine for general maintenance will include weeding, feeding, hoeing, putting support systems in place, sowing annual seeds, bulb planting, planting tender perennials after the last frosts and removing and protecting them before the first, checking for pests and diseases and introducing natural predators to control them. Some of these tasks will need to be done weekly, while others

Heather Aston,
Head Gardener
UPTON HOUSE, WEST
MIDLANDS

From Upton House, as you follow the stripes across the front lawn your eye is drawn to the lines of sweet chestnut (Castanea sativa) *trees in the pasture land ahead, but as you reach the edge, a wonderful terraced garden of mixed borders waits to be explored in the valley below.*

just need your attention once or twice a year. But the more you work and the more time you spend in the border, the more you will see and appreciate the plants around you.

To maintain a healthy stock, shrubs and plants will need to be propagated throughout the year at the optimum times. For example, most shrubs, such as buddleia and rockrose (*Cistus*), can be propagated in early autumn by taking soft-wood cuttings; other shrubs, such as dogwood (*Cornus*) and willow (*Salix*), can be propagated by hard-wood cuttings. Many herbaceous plants, such as asters and achillea, can either be divided in the spring or soft vegetation cuttings taken as growth starts to appear, while some herbaceous plants are better propagated by root cuttings. For instance, anemone root cuttings need to be taken in the autumn and over-wintered indoors before replanting out in the spring as healthy new plants. This will ensure a clean and healthy border throughout the year.

Annual maintenance

Annual maintenance is paramount as it sets the standards for the border for the following year and will also help with soil structure and moisture retention. This is usually done in the winter but you have to bear in mind that some plants might well be winter flowering and some spring bulbs might be early. So when you choose to do it will very much depend on your location and the plants in your border. Here is a checklist of tasks and areas to look at:

Plant maintenance

- **Herbaceous perennials:** removal of dead foliage and support systems, dividing and replanting.
- **Bulbs:** splitting up and replanting.

- **Shrubs:** removal, replanting, pruning to maintain shape and size, removal of diseased, damaged and diverting branches.
- **Trees:** removal of lower laterals and overcrowded, diseased, damaged and diverting branches.
- **Wall shrubs and climbing plants:** prune and train branches to maintain shape and structure.

When the plants have all been pruned into shape the border will then need to be lightly forked over to relieve any soil compaction before applying a generous helping of organic matter spread evenly over the border to a depth of 8cm (3in). Homemade compost is ideal in this situation but any organic matter will do. This is very important in maintaining an open and fibrous soil structure and also maintaining a level of moisture retention for the plants.

Tips

- Establish a good routine of plant husbandry – in other words, do not leave it for several years and then do it all at once!
- Research your plants and get to know what they like before planting. Do they prefer dry or wet conditions, heavy or light soil?
- Keep a diary of maintenance routines, noting dates of planting, feeding, propagating, composting etc.
- Constantly stand back and view the border. There is always room for change and improvement, trying out new planting combinations, such as planting different varieties of clematis around wooden pillars to add height and colour. Pruning shrubs slightly differently can also add a fresh focal point to the border.
- My best advice, after you have done all that, is to sit back and enjoy!

Autumn work in herbaceous borders

First thoughts

Herbaceous borders are the antithesis of the low-maintenance shrub and ground-cover type of garden – but they also rapidly repay the effort that goes into them. As a minimum, they need inspecting and tidying, but autumn is also the season for change and refurbishment. At The Courts, the gardeners walk around together once a month during the year and note the areas that need work on them, so that we have a notebook of ideas by the time September starts. Each year, as well as the regular work of cutting back and tidying, some areas will need renovating, with plants being divided and new plants positioned.

Cutting back

There is a strong case for not cutting back all herbaceous borders in autumn. Here we leave some borders uncut until far into the winter – not only as good hibernating places for beneficial insects, but also to enjoy their company on frosty days, when they develop a magic that can equal their summer heyday.

When we do cut back, we make sure to cut right back to the ground, rather than leave a forest of 8-cm (3-in) stems that dry out and stab the

Cat Saunders,
Head Gardener
THE COURTS
GARDEN, HOLT,
NEAR BRADFORD-
ON-AVON,
WILTSHIRE

Tucked away in the village of Holt, The Courts Garden is a gem of the Arts and Crafts Movement, created on the site of an old woollen mill. Yew and holly hedges divide the garden into separate rooms furnished with the densely planted herbaceous borders for which the garden is famous.

unwary when staking the following spring. If the weather's been wet, we work off planks to avoid compacting the ground any further. Everything that can be is composted – shredded or cut into short lengths before going on the heap. Weeds are removed and the ground is lightly forked over.

Renovating

If we are replanting a large area, we simply dig everything out onto plastic sheets, and cover the roots up with hessian or more plastic. A cool day but not soaking wet is the ideal – if the weather suits a gardener, it will suit the plants and the soil too. We then spread a good 10-cm (4-in) layer of compost over the soil, and fork it in. If we're working on individual plants, we always mix compost into the planting hole, and into the backfilling soil. Herbaceous plants are asked to do a lot so the soil has to be in good heart.

Dividing plants

What to divide? If a plant has become a doughnut with a bare centre (as *Phlox paniculata* will); if it flowers poorly or not at all (we find *Achillea* 'Moonshine' needs a biennial stir up); if it flops quickly; if the foliage looks small and seedy when it should be lush and bold – then the time is ripe for splitting. Some plants are famous for never needing division – day lily (*Hemerocallis*) can labour on for years, as do hostas and cranesbills (*Geranium macrorrhizum*) – but when split will suddenly get an almost teenage lust for life. Others, however, will look at you resentfully when you approach with a fork, like slow to establish gas plant (*Dictamnus alba*) and blue false indigo (*Baptisia australis*), and these should be left alone.

Two forks back to back are good for many plants – they tease the crown apart and keep each division with more of its fibrous roots. Some plants can be pulled apart with your hands, others need a sharp spade, which cuts through some crown buds, but still gives enough to play with. A good sharp, but not serrated, knife will allow the division of tight woody roots such as those of astilbe, especially if the soil is rinsed off under a hose beforehand. If you are contemplating trying to split an overlarge phormium, take an axe with you.

Not everything can be split in autumn – plants of doubtful hardiness (like the border lobelias) should be split in spring. Also, we try to split early in the autumn, so that the new divisions can settle into soil that is still warm. If we leave it later we have more losses.

Planting

Make a large enough hole to take all the roots spread out; this is always a far bigger hole than expected! Backfill with prepared soil and firm in with your hands. Water when all the roots are covered and then carry on backfilling. Plants in pots that look root bound can be snipped with secateurs around the base three times, which encourages more fibrous rooting into the soil. Most are planted with the root ball just covered. Plants such as peony and dicentra, which have resting buds just at soil level, shouldn't be planted too deeply as it inhibits flowering, and can cause the buds to rot over winter.

Tip

Save some seed as you go through your borders – although particular cultivars will not always come true. Collect seed on fine days, laying it out on newspaper until it is thoroughly dry. After cleaning your seed, it can then be stored in a plastic box in the fridge, with silica gel inside to help keep the seed dry.

Gardening by the sea

Coastal gardening

All of us lucky enough to enjoy a sea view from our gardens soon realize that the biggest down side to this ever-changing dramatic landscape is wind. Higher wind velocities accentuated by the exposure to the open sea not only create the problem of establishing any new plants, but in addition water loss through higher transpiration rates, not to mention damage caused by salt scorch and wind-blown sand.

But enough of the negatives, what are the advantages? Apart from the obvious 'stunning views', being close to the sea (in Cornwall's case being almost surrounded) can provide better ambient temperatures due the presence of the warmer body of water, and higher light levels, aided by reflection from the body of water. Armed with the knowledge of both positives and negatives for gardening we are able to make full use of our situation.

Shelter

Shelter is a crucial element for any coastal garden. A good shelter planting will filter the wind and not block it (creating a block can cause an increase in wind velocity by eddying and causing

Ian Wright,
Head Gardener
TRENGWAINTON
GARDEN,
PENZANCE,
CORNWALL

Situated 3.2km
(2 miles) west of
Penzance in Cornwall,
Trengwainton has a
unique series of walled
gardens that are home
to a collection of exotic
plants from the four
corners of the globe.
The terrace at the top
of the garden enjoys
spectacular views out
over Mount Bay to the
Lizard Peninsular.

vortices as the wind is funnelled over the block). A good shelter needs to be planted in layers, filtering the wind by using the plants' differing densities to greatest effect. This is why many artificial shelters or screens are not as effective as plants. Look at how natural planting in the wild adapts to these conditions and this is what we need to replicate in the garden.

Plants shaped by the wind can be three to four times older than their sheltered counterparts. In the south-west we can use a wide range of plants. To achieve protection for larger gardens, a shelter of trees can be used; we use species such as Monterey pine (*Pinus radiate*), Monterey cypress (*Cupressus macrocarpa*) and holm oak (*Quercus ilex*). But just as important is the under planting, which filters at lower levels. This is achieved by using plants such as holly, gorse and sea buckthorn. Within larger gardens or for initial shelter for smaller gardens, plants such as *Griselinia, Olearia, Pittosporum* and *Escallonia* can be used. These could also be used to compartmentalize the inner garden thereby further filtering the wind. When gardening close to the sea in the east, which is exposed to colder winds, the same principle applies, but using a different range of plants, such *Elaeagnus* x *ebbingei* and, from the windy coastal areas of Japan, *Euonymus japonicus*.

Soil

Coastal gardens such as ours have common soil issues that need consideration, for example lack of depth, in conjunction with a very free draining aspect. Hence good soil management is essential when coastal gardening. Incorporating large quantities of organic material regularly will help improve not only the quality of the soil, but also significantly aid its water retention ability. One advantage of being close to the sea means a ready supply of seaweed is usually at hand, with obvious benefits in improving soil nutrient levels.

Planting

Perhaps planting in coastal gardens could be described as a form of hide and seek as new plants are tucked carefully into hidden pockets, away from relentless coastal winds.

In the West Country planting near the coast allows us to let our imaginations run wild and push the boundaries of hardiness. The drier, stony aspects in mild places can even support members of the succulent community, such as *Agave, Aeonium*, ice plant (*Lampranthus*) and *Aloe*. These plants will survive surprisingly low temperatures but not when combined with wet soil conditions. The areas of garden with greater soil depth and quality provide opportunities for plants from countries such as New Zealand, Chile, South Africa and Australia as well as plants from the countries bordering the northern shores of the Mediterranean. *Myrtus, Podocarpus, Drimys, Acacia and Escallonia* can all be grown. If you have a very mild situation and want to give a really exotic feel try *Protea, Banksia, Echium* or members of the palm family, all of which thrive in poor, free-draining, non-cultivated soil.

If you do not want to sacrifice any of your sea view with hedges, look at what grows in your local area naturally that survives and flourishes despite the wind and salinity. Sea thrift (*Armeria maritima*), sea campion (*Silene maritima*) and sea kale (*Crambe maritima*) all adapt well to life near the sea – the clue is in the name and looking at the Latin interpretation will help you to find alternative forms for the garden. Much of our native coastal planting, spectacularly beautiful in its own right, gives a feel of an alpine garden, and indeed many plants from this group will flourish in the similar conditions that are generated by being close to the sea.

Tips

- Planting among stones will aid drainage and the stones themselves will radiate warmth long into the night.
- Incorporating large quantities of organic matter will aid water retention and increase the range of plants that can be grown.
- Look at what grows naturally in your surrounding area. Spend time researching garden forms of these plants to give a larger choice when planning new planting schemes in a challenging situation.
- When planning shelter for your garden use native plants as well as exotics to build up the layers of your shelter.

Fruit and Vegetables

Fruit and Vegetables

Why grow soft fruit?

Few gardening experiences can match the sheer delight of picking fresh fruit you have grown and guzzling as you go. Sure, it takes an age to even cover the bottom of the punnet, let alone fill it, but why take the fun out of gardening? But if you have a more controlled approach to the job and some of the yield does make it back to base, then transforming it into your favourite dessert is pretty good too. A summer pudding, a cream tea or just a bowl of fruit; things don't get much better!

On the other hand, there can be few more forlorn sights than a neglected fruit plot, forgotten bushes choked by brambles and perennial weeds, with mildew and mould in place of succulent fruit. To ensure the former and to minimize the chances of the latter, a modicum of good practice will ensure that you have a sizeable annual crop for years to come.

The choice is yours!

A little market research will soon identify your family's preferences and growing a couple of bushes of each fruit type is a good place to start. Pick some for eating fresh and keep the remainder for processing. Most soft fruit is self-compatible

Steve Biggins,
Head Gardener
CALKE ABBEY,
DERBYSHIRE

Rejuvenated over the last 18th-century walled garden at Calke Abbey is home to an impressive collection of traditional fruit and vegetable varieties grown in a range of sheds, pits, frames and a vinery.

(pollinates itself), but evidence suggests that cropping is improved when cross-pollination is possible.

Strawberries are always popular, but I would like to challenge you to widen your taste experiences and plant gooseberries instead of strawberries. A plump gooseberry left to ripen is syrupy sweet and the gooseberry bush makes for less work than the strawberry patch, which will need renewing quite often. Strawberries are the mainstay of pick-your-own farms and can be found everywhere in summer.

Whitecurrants and redcurrants are a rarity in the shops and you can pay the earth for a tiny punnet the size of a matchbox, so I think space should be allocated for these as well.

Healthy eating is now recognized as a vital constituent of a healthy lifestyle, and with fresh fruit being a rich source of vitamin C, not to mention fibre, a small fruit plot in the back garden should be a priority for most gardeners.

Making a start

Shop around before you buy: bare-rooted plants of a named variety obtained from a reputable fruit nursery are a must. This is a long-term project, so it's worth investing a little time and effort. If you have decided to grow strawberries then they should be certified virus-free stock; in other words avoid the plants potted in yogurt tubs from the bring-and-buy stall at the school fête.

Technical stuff

Fruit bushes and canes should be planted during their period of dormancy, say between December and January, in well-prepared, clean open ground. Ideally soft fruits prefer a slightly acid soil (about pH 6.5), but soil treatment is not necessary unless your soil is very acid (about pH 5.5), in which case lime should be added. Similarly, very chalky soils can cause mineral deficiencies that need to be counteracted by the addition of minerals. As soils will always revert to type and your treatments will need repeating, it's handy to keep a soil-testing kit in your potting shed.

Trowel planting will suffice for strawberries, but bush fruit needs a little more effort. Dig a generous-sized hole and spread the roots of the plant in all directions. While gently shaking the plant, gradually backfill the hole, incorporating copious amounts of garden compost, and firm the plant into position. Mulching with the same material is vital to keep in the moisture of the winter throughout the drier summer months. Leave about a 1.5-m (5-ft) space between plants.

After planting, pruning is key to strong growth during the first season and that means strong growth in the correct position. Get it right now and you've cracked it. Blackcurrants need pruning to 5cm (2in) to encourage all shoots to come from ground level. With redcurrants, whitecurrants and gooseberries the aim is to produce an open goblet-shaped bush on a section of bare stem (or a 'leg'). Commence this by reducing the existing framework by half to an outward facing bud.

You're not finished yet
In mid February when the days are lengthening and the soil warms a little apply a potash-rich top dressing to the base of the plant and top up that mulch. This is the most effective form of weed control and will negate the need for watering. How green is that!

What a pest
Look out for and pick off any small green gooseberry sawfly caterpillars that might invade in April and combat mildew by keeping a nice open bush.

If birds appear to be enjoying more than their share of the spoils, erect a temporary cage with 1–2m (3–6ft) of netting supported by hazel canes or bamboos. If squirrels come calling then all's fair in love and war.

Tips

- Always pick soft fruit in dry weather.
- If you want to grow raspberries, try the autumn-fruiting varieties.
- If your growing space is limited, train cordon gooseberries and whitecurrants or redcurrants up a fence or trellis.

Fruit pruning

The purpose of fruit pruning

In the first years after planting, formative pruning consists of producing a strong framework of branches able to bear good crops in later years. There is an old saying, 'There is no fruit without wood.' It is a good idea to knock off any fruit formed in the first year to channel the tree's energy into the production of strong growth.

The purpose of all fruit pruning is to encourage flower production, which in turn will produce a fine crop of fruit. Most of our garden fruit produces flower on wood made the previous season. At its most fundamental, pruning is calculated to direct the plant's energy into the production of accessible, evenly developed and ripened fruit.

When to prune

Most fruit is best pruned when the sap has receded; January is the ideal month. Remove any dead, diseased or crossing wood from the framework of branches. With apple and pear trees and bushes, in order to space the fruit evenly over the available shoots, the vigour of the most recent branches should be equalized. To do this, assess the average thickness of the young growth. An average

Neil Porteous,
Gardens and Parks
Advisor, Northern
Territory
HEELIS, NATIONAL
TRUST CENTRAL
OFFICE, SWINDON,
WILTSHIRE

There are few pursuits as rewarding as growing and eating your own fruit. Whether your preference is for growing top fruit such as apples or soft fruit such as raspberries, the general principles for pruning the plants are the same.

shoot should be shortened to approximately five buds above the join of the latest wood to that made last season. A weaker shoot should be cut harder to two or three buds and a stronger shoot to seven to nine buds. The harder a shoot is pruned, the stronger it grows back.

With restricted fruit forms such as espalier apples or cordon pears, this equalizing pruning is carried out in mid to late August. The reason for this is to encourage the tree to produce flower buds as near to the join of the old wood as possible. During January, these shoots are further shortened to one or two buds in order to keep these specialist forms compact and neat. Cobnuts and filberts are treated in a similar way, except the summer shortening is called 'brutting' and is done by hand by breaking a vigorous side shoot in half and leaving it to dangle on the tree. The 'brutted' shoots are then shortened again in winter to three or four buds.

Stone top fruit such as plums, cherries, peaches and nectarines are best pruned in spring soon after the new growth begins. All these fruit trees are susceptible to the fungal infection 'silver leaf' if pruned during the winter. They flower on both one-year-old and two-year-old wood with the exception of the peach, which flowers predominantly on one-year-old wood. These fruits are ideally grown as fans where space is limited. This guiding principle for pruning also holds true for most soft fruit: prune out the fruited wood immediately the crop has been taken. This provides light and air into the canopy in order to ripen the young wood for next year's crop of flowers. Blackcurrants, whitecurrants and redcurrants, gooseberries, raspberries, blackberries, hybrid berries (such as tayberries) and blueberries all benefit from winter pruning, which consists of shortening these ripened young shoots to outward-facing buds when the plants are dormant.

Tender fruits, such as figs and vines, are best grown on the protection of a wall. Figs are best pruned in April to prevent frost damage. Thin out the young shoots by cutting each alternate shoot back to one bud to encourage new growth. In the summer each lateral should be 'stopped' at four to five leaves. Take care as fig sap is caustic in sunlight and can cause burns to the skin. Prune from the bottom up using a piece of charcoal as a styptic to reduce the flow of sap. Vines are pruned back to a bud or two of the spurs in December or January. When the growth starts up, rub out all but the best-positioned laterals emanating from each spur. These are stopped one or two leaves after the flowers and tied on to any available support. As the fruit forms, the laterals will sprout again. Rather than rubbing these out completely, stop the sub-laterals at one leaf and so on with each subsequent break. Eventually the diameter of these laterals will be so small that the developing fruit will capture the majority of the sap. Keeping these laterals growing even weakly ensures the flow of sap to the expanding grapes.

Tip

Whatever you are pruning, always dip the blades of your secateurs or knife into a jar of methylated spirit to sterilize them before wiping them down and moving on to another plant.

Plant propagation

Why propagate plants?
If you've got time and a little space, there's
nothing like the feeling of growing something
yourself, whether from seeds or cuttings.

Sowing annual seeds
Annual seeds should be planted from January to
March or April. The tools you will require are:
* 7cm (2¾in) pot or seed tray
* compost (50:50 mix of fine-grade coir and
  propagation bark)
* label and pencil
* propagator

Method
* Use a pot or tray that is suitable for the
  amount of seed you have.
* Fill your container to about three-quarters full
  (do not skimp on compost).
* Use another pot or wooden press to make a
  level, slightly firm surface.
* Sow your seeds evenly onto the surface.
* Use a fine sieve to just cover the seeds.
* Label your seeds.
* Place the pot or tray in a bowl of water to
  soak until the surface looks wet.

Chris Trimmer,
Nursery Supervisor
KNIGHTSHAYES
COURT, TIVERTON,
DEVON

*Knightshayes Court is
a Victorian country
house with richly
decorated interiors and
a celebrated garden. The
Heathcoat Amory
family, our donors, were
passionate about their
garden and added
features such as a
water-lily pool, topiary
hedges, specimen trees
and some truly rare
shrubs. Woodland walks
lead through the
grounds and the newly
restored kitchen garden
contains a vast arrange
of unusual culinary
and herbaceous plants.*

- Place in a propagator with bottom heat set on 21°C (70°F) and do not allow to dry out.
- The seeds should germinate within two weeks.

Aftercare
- Once germinated and the first true leaves have emerged, think about pricking out.
- Gently hold on to the seed leaves. Using a pencil, lift the seedling out of the compost.
- Use good compost (peat free). Make a larger hole with your pencil than you need and then gently place your seedling into the hole and firm in.
- Water in, using a fine spray.
- Finally, check your seedlings. If they have been flattened by watering, use a pencil to gently lift the leaves off the compost. By doing this simple job you can improve the seedlings' chances of survival.

Sowing perennial, shrub, tree and bulb seeds
Seeds of perennials, shrubs, trees and bulbs can be planted at any time of year.

Method
- Prepare compost using one part fine-grade coir peat, one part propagation bark and one part loam.
- Sow as you would annual seeds (see above), then cover with around 3–4mm (⅛–⅙in) of fine gravel.
- Soak for about half an hour.
- Place in a cold frame outside until they germinate. Be prepared to wait. Patience is a virtue – some seeds can take up to three years to germinate.

Aftercare

- Prick out when large enough to handle into small pots (never over-pot seedlings because this is actually detrimental to the plant).
- With tiny seedlings of bulbs or perennials such as primulas, plunge the whole pot into a 1 litre (35fl oz) pot surrounded by compost, for a year. This lets the plant bulk up into good-sized clumps.
- Liquid feed with a seaweed-based fertilizer – a good idea with bulbs as this increases the size of the bulb quickly.

Softwood cuttings

Softwood cuttings can be taken between February and October. The tools you require for the job are:

- safety razor blade
- secateurs
- cuttings compost or peat-free plugs (50:50 mix of fine-grade coir peat or propagation bark)
- rooting powder
- labels
- plastic bag
- propagator

The type of material you obtain for your cutting should be:

- pest and disease free
- juvenile material (fresh new growth)
- true to type (i.e. if it's variegated, make sure the cutting is variegated)
- at least 5–8cm (2–3in) long

Method

- Use a plastic bag – damp inside to stop your cuttings drying out.
- Look over the plant you want to propagate. Check the material – if it's too soft leave it for a few days and try again. It is best if the stem is slightly firm to the touch.
- Use secateurs to cut just above a leaf joint. The cutting should be at least 5–8cm (2–3in) long. Place in the bag.
- Try to prepare it as soon as possible.
- Remove from the bag. Use your safety razor blade to make the first cut just below a leaf joint 5–8cm (2–3in) from the top of the cutting. Make sure it's a flat, clean cut.
- Remove some of the leaves further up the stem, leaving the buds intact. Remove enough leaves to insert a good 2.5cm (1in) into the plug/compost.
- Gather the leaves at the top together and cut in half. This reduces water loss from the cutting.
- Insert the base of the cutting into hormone rooting powder. Tap off any excess.
- Insert the cutting gently into the compost.
- Water in and label.
- Place in a humid atmosphere with bottom heat set at 21°C (70°F). A small electric propagator is fine. Keep out of direct sunlight and mist several times a day.

The cuttings should start to root within two weeks. You can usually tell when they start to show signs of growing. Don't be tempted though, to pot them on straight away. Your new plants have been used to the good life and have to be weaned gradually by slowly opening the vents and letting the outside world in. This process should take a week or so.

Finally, after about three to four weeks, you can gently pot up your new plants and reflect on the fact that you have some new plants without a trip to a garden centre.

Tips for seed sowing

- Always use fresh seeds.
- Don't let the seed pots dry out too much.
- Remember to label well as you can guarantee you will forget what you have planted three years down the line.

Tips for softwood cuttings

- Try to take the cuttings in the morning before it gets too warm.
- Make sure you have everything ready before you take your cuttings.
- Just have a go; you'll be surprised what you can achieve.

In the kitchen garden

There are few more satisfying aspects of gardening than literally reaping the fruits (and vegetables) of your labours. From sun-warmed strawberries to the earliest asparagus, home grown is impossible to beat. The advantage of growing your own is that you are in control of what goes into the production of the crop. No matter what the scale of your garden there is usually space for some fruit and vegetables.

Keep ahead of the opposition

There is a great thrill in gathering the first of any crop. What about considering the benefits of earlier crops by taking advantage of cloches, greenhouses and forcing jars, as well as any microclimates produced by walls?

Cloches will give shelter from both the weather and pests, and can be used for fruit and vegetables to stagger your crop.

However, if this is not possible on your plot consider sowing your seed in sectioned trays or pots; the resulting plants can then be planted out when the weather is suitable. These trays can be given the shelter of a greenhouse or frame but care should be taken to avoid bringing them on too early as bad weather can delay planting out

Christine Brain, Head Gardener
BARRINGTON COURT, SOMERSET

The kitchen garden at Barrington Court has been cultivated continuously since its creation by Colonel A A Lyle in 1921. Its enclosing walls are covered with trained fruit and the wide range of fruit and vegetables produced are now used in the National Trust restaurant.

into the garden, leading to checking of the young plants – so don't be too impatient.

Forcing jars can be used for rhubarb, sea kale and chicory to obtain early spring vegetables. All of these benefit from the exclusion of light to blanch the stems, meaning that the tender young shoots emerge earlier.

Everyone knows the benefits of south-facing walls to give protection to tender plants including peaches, nectarines and apricots, and to bring blossom out earlier as well as creating sheltered beds at the foot of the wall.

But equally north walls can hold back the blossom of fruit, enabling early blossom that might be susceptible to frosts to be delayed. This is particularly useful with plums, gages and damsons. Crops planted at the base of these walls will also be delayed so this is also a great way of extending the harvesting season.

Autumn-sown vegetables such as Japanese onions, broad beans and peas are hardy and can survive outside throughout the winter months, maturing to give early crops in the spring.

Pests

With the movement away from using chemicals on crops, full advantage should be taken of any natural help available to counter pests in the garden:

- Grow flowers to attract beneficial insects.
- Grow resistant seed varieties, such as parsnips that are resistant to canker.
- Plan the sowing of your seeds to avoid peak pest times, for example make repeat sowings of early carrots to avoid carrot root fly.
- Improve moisture levels to deter pests, such as flea beetle on brassicas.
- Use physical barriers to help with pests of all shapes and sizes.
- Consider using fine mesh to keep butterflies away from brassicas and coarser mesh to keep birds away from fruit.

Staggering your crops

- When a crop is in the ground consider what can be planted next to make maximum use of the plot.
- To avoid problems with gluts of one crop, sow small amounts of seed at regular intervals.
- Make use of transplanted thinnings, which will often mature later than those left in place, especially lettuce.
- Start seeds again in sectioned trays or pots before the previous crop has been harvested. These can give you a head start in fast germination and enable the small seedlings to grow away quickly without competition from weeds that can be such a problem early in the year.

A milder climate

Take advantage of the current milder weather conditions to experiment with some of the more tender varieties outdoors. In a good summer aubergines, peppers, tomatillos and Cape gooseberries will all produce good crops in favourable sites. Be brave, have a go. You'll be amazed by what you can grow!

Tips

- Pete Belben, who is in charge of the Kitchen Garden at Barrington Court, gives the best advice going – 'Don't fight nature!'
- Wait until the weather conditions are correct.
- Taking care of the soil is the key to successful gardening.

Green Gardening

Making compost

Why we needed compost

Serious compost making started at Anglesey Abbey in 1999 in an attempt to address the difficulties caused through increased drought periods; we wanted to make a usable product from the 40 hectares (98 acres) of the garden, knowing that this would assist in retaining water in our very free-draining soil; we now recycle 95 per cent of garden waste.

Benefits of compost making

Every garden produces garden waste and it is possible to turn almost all of it back into a useful product, bringing benefits to the long-term good of the soil, plants and ecology systems by adding compost or mulch layers to the soil surface. Benefits of compost making include the following:

- The increase of moisture retention, reduction in evaporation rates and the aiding of penetration of natural rainfall, which particularly benefit dry areas of the garden.
- The addition of mild nutrients and assistance in aerating the soil through the increased action of worms and other insects. Micro-organisms introduced through the addition

Richard Todd,
Head Gardener
ANGLESEY ABBEY
GARDENS, LODE,
CAMBRIDGE

The gardens of Anglesey Abbey are situated on the Fen Edge of Cambridgeshire and were created with the influence of the first Lord Fairhaven. The garden includes something for every season in the Herbaceous Border, Dahlia Garden, Formal Garden and the Winter Garden.

of compost can assist the release of nutrients that otherwise remain locked up in the soil.

- Suppression of weed development when added as a mulch layer, protection of surface roots and assistance in promoting the best soil temperature during hot summers.

What is needed to make compost?

The actual making of compost is not complicated or difficult; we make up to 60m³ (2,000ft³) a year. There are four basic ingredients that are needed in any sized compost heap, which are green waste, brown waste, air and water. A suitable site, bin or bunker system will, of course, also be needed to carry out the full process.

Green waste (nitrogen rich)

This is basically any plant (with the exception of invasive weeds) that is still green or fleshy; this is the vital activator for any compost making. This material when heaped will begin to break down fast and produce heat quickly. It could include grass clippings, old flower heads or stems and any shredded foliage. Do not make heaps of pure green waste as it must be mixed with other materials such as brown waste.

Brown waste (carbon rich)

This is any part of a plant that is basically brown, including autumn leaves, woody shredded material from shrub pruning but not woodchips. Woodchips will take much longer to break down; we make a separate heap for this product. Cardboard packaging and shredded paper can also be added in small amounts.

Air

The amount of air within the mix is essential to create the correct environment for aerobic action to begin; this action creates heat that then promotes the breakdown of materials. Too much green waste, such as a lot of grass clippings at one time will block out the air and promote the wrong type of bacteria, which smell very bad.

Regular turning of heaps is essential both to keep air in the mix and thoroughly mix up the greens and browns as there is a danger that layers of material can remain untouched. During the life of an average heap we would aim to turn it at least six times. Fortunately for us we have the use of a tractor with a fore-end loader to assist this process. It is also important to manage the site so that there is sufficient space or a spare bin or bunker into which to turn the heap.

Water

In an ideal world, by using the correct ratio of green to brown, which for us is approximately 60 to 40 per cent split, you do not need to add any extra water. When insufficient green material is available it is necessary to add water as a dry heap will remain inactive. A dry heap cannot create enough heat and so the possibility of breaking down material that may include some weed seeds will decrease. We find that covering the whole heap with black polythene proves to be a good way of reducing heat loss.

Tips

- Do not add plant material carrying persistent disease; also avoid adding any cooked food waste, which may attract vermin.
- Invasive weeds with fleshy roots, such as bindweed, couch grass and ground elder, can be made harmless by putting them into a black plastic bag, leaving them to rot down for some weeks and then adding them to the heap.

Hedges for habitats

Wildlife in hedgerows

Heritage gardens are increasing in significance for wildlife, partly in response to habitat loss in the countryside, and partly on account of our enhanced perception. Hedges figure strongly in both these aspects. The loss of hedges from the farmed landscape is well known, but only those of us who have experienced the dawn chorus in a well-hedged garden will begin to appreciate the ramifications. Garden hedges offer far more to wildlife than nesting sites for beleaguered song birds, though much depends on the hedge's species composition and physical structure. There is, of course, a limit to the number of song bird territories a garden can support: the quality and quantity of potential nesting sites is only one feature of a detailed matrix.

The invertebrate fauna of garden hedges is undoubtedly vast, but our knowledge is restricted to a few salient species like the holly blue butterfly. A hedge will support insects and other invertebrates that feed on or in the foliage, flowers, buds and stems – plus a veritable pestilence of other invertebrates that are parasitic or predatory upon those rather innocuous plant feeders. Indeed, the spider fauna at Blickling Hall,

*Matthew Oates,
Advisor on Nature
Conservation*
HEELIS, NATIONAL
TRUST CENTRAL
OFFICE, SWINDON,
WILTSHIRE

In childhood I scrambled among the ancient yew hedges of Montacute in Somerset, searching for birds' nests. The magic of that secret world has since intensified: those convoluted yews reveal more wildlife and associated issues than a boy could possibly imagine.

Norfolk, and the yew colossi at Montague House, Somerset, could be quite rich, but we simply do not know.

Hedges and walls provide shelter from wind and, crucially, enhance micro-climate conditions. These factors benefit a host of winged insects that cannot function in wind, or need intense warmth. Thus, winged insects migrate from the land and lakes surrounding Sissinghurst into the garden, where they add an extra dimension to an already sublime garden experience. Essentially, the hedges function as a surrogate woodland-edge habitat, and a great many insects are creatures of sheltered wood edges. The Arts and Crafts Movement must have benefited these creatures wonderfully!

In addition, another world exists at the bottom of the hedge, where litter decomposes; or rather, where litter is decomposed by fungal organisms and myriad invertebrates, which are heavily impeded by their own predators and parasites. Here, of course, the aptly-named hedgehog feeds, and may even over-winter in safety.

Half the mammal fauna of lowland Britain commonly use hedges, including garden hedges. Ask your cat, or observe how cats patrol along hedges, mainly in search of small mammals. And at night, bats will hunt for insects flying in the lea of taller hedges. Recently, it has been found that the dormouse readily uses thick mixed hedges, which hold plenty of buds in spring and berries in autumn, both important seasonal food sources.

Choosing your hedging

The simple truth is that any garden hedge will benefit wildlife to a modest or great extent, even low edging. It is a win-win-win situation. But, as in life outside the garden, much depends on our objectives and what we allow to happen, or seek to prevent. Obviously, biodiversity can be optimized by establishing varied hedges of mixed species composition.

The definitive wildlife garden hedge would include evergreens for shelter, spring and summer flowering shrubs that also bear berries in autumn and winter, climbers such as ivy and honeysuckle, and, interestingly, both native and non-native plant species. Of course, the range and permutations are already nearly endless, and these are likely to alter considerably under climate change: milder winters should facilitate the cultivation of more non-native shrubs, though summer drought may impede establishment or reduce longevity, and there is the dark shadow of increased diseases. Once again, we are spoilt for choice. Overleaf is a selection of tips that seek to help both gardeners and wildlife.

Tips

- Be kind to hedgehogs, leaf-litter invertebrates, yourself and the hedge: push minor hedge trimmings under the hedge, and leave them to rot.
- Encourage the holly blue butterfly, that azure jewel of spring and late summer, by growing flowering holly and flowering ivy: the caterpillars feed on the buds of these plants. Ivy flowers are great for autumn insects, and the berries of both plants are favoured by birds. Any flowering cultivars will do.
- Establish a buddleia hedge, perhaps around greenhouses to provide summer shade. All *Buddleia davidii* cultivars attract myriad butterflies, moths and bees. The best is called *B. davidii* 'Beijing', but it is only available from certain butterfly farms and wildflower specialists.
- Bring back the lavender hedge! These are fantastic for bees and cabbage white butterflies – but watch out for your cabbages.
- Don't trim hedges during the bird nesting season, obviously – it's surprising how many people do.
- The much-abused 'Leyland Cypress' (*Cupressocyparis leylandii* hybrids) makes an excellent hedge, beloved by nesting and roosting birds. It needs cutting only once a year, in autumn or winter.

Peat-free growing

Why peat?

Peat is a naturally occurring organic material that is completely inert. It holds moisture well and evenly; add fertilizer and it becomes a fantastic growing medium that is always consistent. Its use in horticulture has grown up largely over the last 40 to 50 years. Since peat-based composts were developed, the use of container-grown plants has become very popular, whereas previously most plants were sold bare rooted. Container-grown plants are much easier to sell both wholesale and retail and plants can now be sold all year round. Since the modernization of peat-based compost the amateur gardening market has grown enormously.

Why peat free?

Almost 90 per cent of peat bog habitats have been lost over the last century. Peat bogs are among the most delicate habitats in the world and are home to a large diversity of wildlife, both flora and fauna. The destruction of this habitat has been largely due to the demands of horticulture with two-thirds of peat extracted in the UK for horticulture used by amateur gardeners. Peat bogs occur all over Europe, including the British Isles,

Alexis Datta,
Head Gardener
SISSINGHURST
CASTLE GARDENS,
SISSINGHURST,
KENT

Vita Sackville-West and her husband Harold Nicolson bought Sissinghurst in 1930 and created the now-famous garden there. At Sissinghurst we grow nearly all the plants we need for the garden ourselves, including annuals, biennials, half hardies, herbaceous perennials and shrubs. We have two glasshouses and an extensive frame yard.

especially Ireland and Scotland, with some in England. If you would like
to see a peat bog you could visit the National Trust's beautiful Wicken Fen
Nature Reserve in Cambridgeshire.

Peat bogs also absorb and store carbon dioxide from the atmosphere.
Continuous exploitation means that this stored CO_2 is being released
and is adding to the global-warming problem.

Experimenting with 'peat free'

For wildlife and environmental reasons, the National Trust has not been using
peat in its gardens since 2000. Sissinghurst was among a number of gardens
chosen to experiment with different peat-free potting composts. Coco fibre
or coir, a by product of coconut production, was leading the way at first. But
further environmental concerns started to surface, as it did not seem viable
to transport coco fibre from the tropics where it is grown, all the way to
Northern Europe to be made into potting compost. There are similar
concerns with wood waste, a by product of foresting, since to be truly 'green'
it is necessary to be sure your waste is sourced from sustainable forestry.
Wood waste and 'green waste' (such as cuttings and compost) need to rot
down before being made into a potting medium. The process of rotting uses
nitrogen, which your plants need to grow.

Having tried many blends, our propagator at Sissinghurst is happiest with
a potting compost made from forestry industry waste, a mix of compost, bark
and wood waste. Some peat-free products tend to be rather lumpy, so for
seeds and cuttings we make our own mixture from commercially available
sifted bark and wood materials.

Using a new type of potting compost is difficult for all gardeners, since
all growing media have their own habits. You have to get used to the way
compost looks; sometimes it is hard to tell if the plants need watering as the

compost may look dry on the top when in fact the roots are quite damp. Learn to look at the plants themselves to tell if they need watering or feeding. The leaves can actually take on a different hue if their roots are dry and of course the plants start to wilt. Alternatively, try picking up the pot to test the weight of the compost and to see if the bottom of the pot is damp.

What will grow?

We find all the large plants we grow do well in the compost we now use. The only really troublesome plants are those that favour acid soils, especially ericaceous subjects, such as azaleas, but for these there are specialist peat-free composts available.

In the garden

Our soil at Sissinghurst is just on the acid side of neutral and as we do not grow many ericaceous plants in the garden we do not need to lower the pH of the soil by adding peat. Saying that, we do have an azalea bank and in the area of the garden called Delos, some rhododendrons do quite well without our trying very hard.

To enhance our rather heavy soil, we dig in lots of compost from our own compost heaps. Some areas we mulch with chipped bark, and again this should not alter the pH of the soil. If you have neutral or alkaline soil, stick to growing plants that will tolerate those conditions, as you will probably find this the most rewarding.

Problems

Really there are no great problems with growing plants in peat-free composts once you have got used to it. Sometimes you will suffer with a pest called sciarid fly. These tiny black flies hover over the compost and you can see them walking on the surface. The minute grubs of these flies feed on the wood waste in the potting compost, but unfortunately they will also make a meal of tender young roots. You can use a biological control such as hyoaspis to kill off the adults and you can also buy yellow sticky strips to catch them.

Tips

- Choose compost made from sustainable forestry wood chips or bark.
- Learn to recognize by look, feel or weight when your plants need water. Do not over water.
- Occasionally, sciarid fly occur in poor-quality composts, so be aware. Use sticky yellow traps hung low near the plants to help control sciarid fly or try a biological control.

Environmentally friendly pest and disease controls

An historical battle

Man's battle with the pests and diseases that compete with him for food crops and ornamental plants is historical. Over the centuries tried and tested methods for the prevention or treatment of these pests and diseases have been handed down from generation to generation. It was not until the mid-20th century however that the armoury of chemicals emerging from the test laboratories of two world wars was found to provide, as a by product, weapons that could also be used to actually 'tame' nature.

Half a century later, the effects of some of those chemicals still persist in our soils and ground-water systems – and therefore in the food chain – and this has provoked the ongoing review and subsequent withdrawal of many harmful pesticides, and a movement back towards the more organic practices used in times past.

Contemporary thinking encourages working with nature, rather than fighting it, and many of the 'greener' garden products coming on to the market reflect this. These days most gardeners employ a combination of techniques both ancient and modern for pest and disease control, and some of these are discussed below.

Lin Ewart,
Horticultural
Technician,
Gardens and Parks
HEELIS, NATIONAL
TRUST CENTRAL
OFFICE, SWINDON,
WILTSHIRE

The National Trust looks after one of the greatest collections of historic gardens and cultivated plants in the world, encompassing more than 400 years of history. The National Trust's central gardens and parks advisory team provides expertise in gardens and parks conservation and oversees standards of care and presentation.

Help your plants to help themselves

A healthy soil containing a thriving population of micro-flora is quite literally the foundation of strong and healthy plant growth.

The incorporation of plenty of organic matter, such as homemade garden compost, well-rotted leaf litter or farmyard manure, will ensure a rich source of biological soil activity, which, in turn, will form a reciprocal relationship with the root systems of your garden plants. This symbiotic process aids the uptake of nutrition and water essential for healthy plant growth, leading to enhanced in-built resistance to attack from pests and diseases.

A sick or lifeless soil simply cannot support healthy plant life, and boosting plant growth by applying 'quick fix' artificial fertilizers does not provide a sustainable solution: used in the long term they can have a detrimental effect on the more desirable and naturally occurring beneficial soil fungi.

To re-establish the life force in poor, compacted or tired soils, dig in plenty of good organic matter on a regular basis, or try some of the growing media products now available on the market that already incorporate beneficial soil organisms (these are called mycorrhizae). It is always worth checking that any such micro-organisms you may introduce to your soil are from a native UK source, as these products are now available.

Encourage wildlife into your garden

Work with nature by gardening as organically as possible. By learning about local wildlife and introducing their living requirements to your garden, you will be rewarded with a variety of insects, birds and animals taking up residence and this, in turn, will help to keep garden-pest populations in check.

When the balance of nature is interrupted, a pest or disease can very quickly take advantage and become a problem. Planting a wide selection of different, nectar-rich plants will attract a greater variety of insects, making it difficult for any one insect population to dominate and reach unmanageable levels.

'Green' products

The gap in the market left by ongoing pesticide withdrawals has prompted the arrival of several 'greener' products based on naturally occurring substances such as garlic, seaweed, citrus extracts and plant oils. These gentler products can be used as a back up to deal with 'hotspots' of infestation or infection as necessary, but have the added bonus of being safer not only for the user, children and household pets, but also for wildlife and the environment generally.

Biological controls

The principle of biological control is based on the natural order taking place all the time in your garden, where the flora and fauna maintain their own equilibrium via the food-chain process.

Biological control of pests, especially under glass, can be achieved by the strategic introduction of a relevant predator into the affected area. Once established, the predator will soon start to reproduce, using the pest population as a food source and reducing it to more manageable proportions.

For a truly sustainable solution, it is important that a certain number of the original pests remain *in situ* in order to provide a continuing food source. In this way both pest and predator can coexist in a controlled environment, and at a population level that the plant crop can tolerate.

Glasshouse pests that can be controlled using biological controls include aphid, red spider mite, whitefly, mealy bug, thrips, slugs, sciarid fly and vine weevils.

Tips

- It is important to read the instructions on the packet in which your biological control arrives before opening it: observe the temperature and living requirements that the predators need to survive in order to do their job for you.
- Above all else, make sure the glasshouse door, windows and vents are shut before you release your predators from their container.

Weed control without chemicals

Clearing uncultivated ground

If you are starting a planting scheme from scratch, clear the ground completely by digging it and removing all weeds as you progress. If possible, planting a 'cleaning crop' is of great benefit and potatoes are the perfect solution. In their cultivation you have to move the soil three times and the dense canopy of leaves on potato plants prevents further weeds from establishing.

Hoeing

Regular hoeing is of prime importance even if there are no obvious signs of weed seedlings. The effect of hoeing is the same as providing soil mulch. A Dutch hoe is best in these circumstances although it is a tool that requires skill to use; start at one end and work backwards with a to-and-fro movement so that the end result is neat rows and you do not walk over what has been hoed. With a draw hoe, a forward chopping movement is used so that the hoed area is walked over, running the risk of trampling weeds back into the soil.

Mulching

Mulches are used to exclude light and prevent weeds germinating. There are many choices.

Barry Champion, Head Gardener
TRELISSICK GARDEN, FEOCK, NEAR TRURO, CORNWALL

Beautifully positioned at the head of the Fal River, Trelissick Garden commands panoramic estuary views. In recent years, environmental awareness has come to the fore and here at Trelissick, to increase our diversity in the garden, a more chemical-free environment has been established. One area we have looked at is the control of weeds without the use of chemicals.

- Black polythene is a very satisfactory inorganic medium for the suppression of annual seedlings and is the most effective mulch to eradicate perennial weeds, but is not attractive if exposed. Biodegradable polythene works in the same way as black polythene but in theory will decay and can then be rotavated or dug back into the soil after cropping. For aesthetic reasons, I would not recommend this for use in an ornamental garden unless an organic mulch was put on top. Confine biodegradable polythene to the vegetable garden.
- Stone and slate chippings are acceptable in some flower gardens but are not as effective as organic mulches.
- Newspapers can be used as organic mulch, mainly in kitchen gardens. Any mulch remaining can be dug into the soil after cropping. Newspapers are not that successful a method.
- Homemade compost is good, although, depending upon the ingredients it might be better reserved for use in the soil rather than on top. It might contain a certain amount of weed seed unless very well made.
- Grass mowings need to be quite deep in order to be effective; they tend to rot anaerobically, becoming smelly and slimy. They are better used in compost rather than as a mulch.
- Farmyard manure is an excellent mulch but can also contain large quantities of weed seeds.
- Mushroom compost contains lime and should not be used on ericaceous plants. Apart from that, it is visually and aesthetically very good as well as being free of weed seeds.
- Wood chips and shredded prunings are excellent mulches but are best if they have been composted for two or three years first. Direct use around objects is fine but the mulch will have to be supplemented with a fertilizer that is high in nitrogen to replace nitrogen lost during decomposition.

- Bark is the most aesthetically pleasing of all mulches. Completely free of weed seeds, different grades can be used for different requirements. It has one major disadvantage – its high cost.
- Leaf mould is the most important mulch in a woodland garden, although it is primarily best for potting composts. Ericaceous plants thrive in it. It is, after all, nature's mulch.
- Peat also is a traditional mulch and soil conditioner, but its use is no longer environmentally acceptable.

Ground cover

Ground cover is an excellent method of suppressing weed growth although you have to remember that some subjects can be very invasive. It is especially important to avoid plants that can escape to the countryside and cause environmental problems (see www.defra.gov.uk for more information). This method can be aesthetically very pleasing.

Tip

When in the garden and you have forgotten your garden twine, there's no need to panic. If you grow any phormiums or cordylines pull off one of the dead leaves and from the base of the leaf tear it up into strips and use to tie up your plants. These ties work perfectly because they decompose in 12 months and don't harm the plants.

Using local reclaimed wood in your garden

While working on the restoration of the garden at Standen, we have discovered a wonderful collection of rare plants from the early 20th century, and overgrown beds and borders that used to overflow with herbaceous perennials, tropical plants and annuals.

As well as the work in the garden we wanted to revive our areas of ancient woodland on the estate and reintroduce coppicing and other traditional management techniques.

There are a plethora of products available commercially to support floppy herbaceous plants, prop up trees and protect newly planted areas, but as our woodland was producing suitable material in abundance, we thought we ought to use this.

Coppiced wood in your garden

I realize very few people have their own woodland to raid for pea sticks and the like; so for many, a nearby source will need to be found. However, these once-essential horticultural items have virtually all fallen out of favour in recent decades. The consequence of this is that much of our woodland is becoming neglected, and bluebells, cowslips, yellow archangel and the high

James Masters,
Head Gardener
STANDEN, EAST
GRINSTEAD, SUSSEX

Standen is an intricate garden of many compartments overlooking the High Weald. Under-resourced for many years, its restoration is aiming to ensure that the garden is once again thoroughly rooted in its local environment, and embraces its creator James Beale's aspiration for sustainability.

brown fritillary butterfly among many, many other flora and fauna, are suffering due to neglect of ancient coppice.

Coppicing trees by cutting to the ground every 7 to 30 years not only provides traditional habitat for a wide range of flora and fauna, but can also increase the lifespan of the coppiced tree by up to ten times and provides a wealth of products for use in the garden.

Pea sticks

These are fan-shaped branches, usually of hazel, which, as the name suggests, are great for supporting both edible and sweet peas. They can also be made into cages, easily woven together around herbaceous plants by late April at an appropriate height, to provide support that will withstand the severest of summer weather. At the end of the season, sticks and perennial tops can all be gathered up and put through the shredder, without the need to untangle metal or plastic or save expensive bamboo canes (see chippings, page 114).

Beanpoles

Generally 2.5–5cm (1–2in) thick, these provide a strong support for anything from runner beans to clematis and can help train roses into trees. Their rough surface provides plenty of opportunities for the plants to get a grip and greatly reduces the need for tying in.

Stakes and poles

These are used to support larger plants, including young trees. Chestnut stakes are strong, reliable and will last up to 20 years in the ground; plenty of time for the plant to establish itself. Y-shaped stakes or stroods can be used to support leaning trees or branches overburdened with fruit.

Hurdles

Generally made from woven hazel, but occasionally also ash, these are usually available in 1.80-m (6-ft) lengths, and at different heights can act as screens and windbreaks, and provide winter protection for tender plants and edgings around borders. You could even try weaving your own *in situ* to follow the curve of a border or plant.

Besom brooms

Far more effective than rakes or brushes for clearing paths, brushing top dressing into lawns (and apprentice witches and wizards), these brooms made from birch or heather can become a firm favourite after just a few minutes of getting accustomed to using them.

Chippings

Any material not suitable for converting into another product can be chipped and used for surfacing paths or as a good, weed-suppressing mulch on borders. As a mulch it is also very good at retaining water in the soil and wood chip will not blow around causing mess, unlike chips of bark.

Other coppiced woodland products

These are just a few of the coppiced woodland products available to use in your garden. Among many others are: arbours, arches and sculptures, fencing and gates, trugs, planters and even charcoal for your barbeque.

Have a look around your local area for coppice woodland products. Although they might not be as readily available as the imported artificial alternative, these tried and tested products with a history of generations of use in gardens will help sustain our ancient woodlands, and maybe with enough demand even help create new ones. You will also be benefiting wildlife and promoting local rural jobs. At Standen, we have helped to ensure the continued survival and regeneration of our woodland by looking nearby first when we require something for the garden.

Tip

- If you can't find what you need in your area, see if there is a local volunteer group working in woodland that you may be able to join and possibly cut your own timber. Also, speak to local gardeners and allotment holders to find out where they obtain their products.

Companion planting

What is companion planting?

Companion planting is a way to ensure that plants can benefit from their neighbours in many different ways. They can be used for ornamental purposes or in the production of food for consumption; there are many plant combinations that can be used from providing a support for climbing plants to attracting beneficial insects that prey on pests. This system can be used by organic and non-organic gardeners and growers alike.

Companion planting has been used since at least Roman times and it has been practised by Native American peoples in a technique known as the Three Sisters, where maize (corn), a climbing bean and squash are all planted together. The way this works is that the maize is used as poles for climbing by the beans and the squash is used as a ground cover mulch to help keep in the moisture under its large leaves.

Today we use all sorts of combinations of planting to confuse the harmful insects and disguise the smell of the plants or crops we are growing. Plants that might be used for combination planting are as follows:

* Plants that give off a scent or chemical that repels insects.

Danny Snapes, Gardener-in-Charge
FENTON HOUSE, HAMPSTEAD, LONDON

Situated in one of the North London suburbs just 150m (164yd) away from the Hampstead Tube station, Fenton House is set in the village area giving Hampstead one of its green oases. The house is set in a completely walled garden with different levels, and is planted for interest from spring to autumn.

- Plants that attract beneficial insects, such as ladybird larvae, parasitic wasps, hoverfly and lacewings.
- Plants that leave a residual chemical in the ground that repels nematodes or benefits the companion plant.
- Plants (such as members of the legume family) that fix nitrogen into the soil via the roots, which are dug in after harvesting.
- Plants benefiting from the same soil and growing conditions that can be happily planted together.
- Plants that create shade for other plants that need shelter from the sun.
- Sacrificial plants that will hopefully attract harmful insects away from certain plants or crops.
- Plants that act as a windbreak for other plants.
- Plants that attract pollinating insects to improve yield of crops.

What types of combinations are possible?

One of the most common combinations is that of roses under-planted with garlic, which gives off a scent that is said to repel aphids. One that is used in the vegetable garden is golden feverfew (*Tanacetum parthenium* 'Aureum') to ward off onion and carrot fly. When I thin out either of these vegetables I rub the feverfew to give off the strong scent, both before and afterwards, to confuse the flies and disguise the smell of the plants. It seems to work as I have never yet had problems with either pest. The bonus of planting the feverfew is that it makes the vegetable garden look good as well.

I have also used Mexican marigold (*Tagetes minuta*), which is around 1.2m (4ft) high, to ward off aphids but have found that it is good for root crops as it gives off a chemical that repels nematodes. It also gives good protection to other plants as a windbreak and to plants that need shade.

I regularly use broad beans as a sacrificial crop as they readily attract aphids early on in the season (but you still get a crop from the beans). This allows me to destroy the aphids by cultural methods, reducing the numbers early on and giving a benefit to the garden for the rest of the season.

I use part of the Native American Three Sisters technique by planting sweet corn and squash in adjacent rows, which helps to keep the moisture in for the corn and also keeps weeds down. In the future I plan to try beans climbing up the stems of the sweet corn as well.

Plants used for companion planting

Common fruit, herbs and vegetables

Plant name	Companions	Incompatible
apple	chives, mint, nasturtiums	
beetroot	beans, onions	runner beans
beans	carrots, cauliflower	onion family, peas
broccoli	broad beans, caraway, dill, potatoes, rosemary, thyme	
cabbage	beans, herbs, celery, beetroot, spinach, Swiss chard	mustard species, onion family

Plant name	Companions	Incompatible
carrots	peas, lettuce, onion family, sage, tomatoes	
courgette	borage, fennel, nasturtium	
garlic	carrots, beetroot, roses, lettuce, tomatoes	beans, peas
leek	celery, carrots, apples, pears	lettuce, parsley
lettuce	carrots, celery, radish, kohlrabi	
onion	tomatoes, parsnips, carrots	beans, peas
pears	mint, nasturtiums	
peas	beans, carrots, radish, turnips, sweet corn	onion family
potato	lavender, horseradish★	sunflowers, sweet corn
sweet corn	squash, beans, pumpkins, sunflower	tomatoes
strawberries	beans, lettuce	rosemary, thyme
tomato	basil, onion family, nasturtiums, marigold, carrot, parsley	potatoes, cabbage family

★ You need to dig horseradish up every year as it is a thug and will spread very quickly.

Flowers and herbs

Plant name	Companions	Incompatible
allium	vegetables, fruit trees, peppers	peas, beans
basil	tomatoes, parsley	tansy, rue
borage	strawberry, squash, tomatoes	
catmint	aubergine, swede, thyme	
coriander	all vegetables, attracts bees	
feverfew	roses, onions, carrots	
geranium	roses, grapevines	
hyssop	cabbage family, grapes	radish
lavender	potatoes, thyme	lettuce, parsley
marigolds	most plants, especially beans, basil, roses, tomatoes	
mustard	cabbage, cauliflower	
nasturtium	apples, pears, radish, cabbage, tomatoes	broad beans
oregano	brassicas	
parsley	asparagus, tomatoes, roses, basil	lavender
rosemary	beans, cabbage, sage, carrots	marrow family
sage	cabbage family, rosemary	cucumbers
thyme	cabbage, beans, roses	marrow family
wormwood	cabbage family, some aromatic herbs	sage, basil
yarrow	most aromatic herbs	

Tips

- When planning a new border think about diversity and companion planting to make it difficult for harmful insects to find the plants that they need for food or to reproduce. One example is planting vegetables and herbs in your decorative borders to confuse the pests and make it more difficult for them to find their food source. This can be very attractive too, as some of the new vegetable plants can look really good.
- Ensure that the plants are growing in the best possible conditions available as this will assist them in fighting off any pests and disease.
- Remember to mulch regularly, weed when needed to stop competition from other plants and fertilize at the right time to ensure that your plants take up the nutrients when most beneficial.

Gardening in a changing climate

While debate about climate changes rages in the media, gardeners are faced with real, tangible changes in weather patterns that affect our work significantly. For several years we have had periods of intense summer heat without precipitation, violent pulses of rain and winters without prolonged periods of frost.

A significant element of the plant collection at Nymans is not adapted to thrive in our current climate. Rhododendrons from the Himalaya need cold, dry winters and cool summers with consistent, but not torrential, rainfall. We have watched mature specimens regress rapidly over the last three years due to winter water logging and summer daytime temperatures of 35°C (95°F) and more.

Simply coping with the changing climate is not enough. National Trust gardens have a tradition of excellence that must continue regardless of the weather. Visitors come to gain inspiration and guidance from us and we must present gardens that are thriving. We use three techniques at Nymans to adapt positively to climate change: water harvesting, reduced watering and plant selection.

Ed Ikin,
Head Gardener
NYMANS, WEST
SUSSEX

One of the great 20th-century gardens, Nymans is a rare combination of beautiful design and an extraordinary plant collection. Botanical rarities grow among dramatic topiary and statues and dazzling displays of annuals. The green gardening techniques employed at Nymans allow the garden to flourish in a changing climate.

Water harvesting

A simple system for water harvesting was installed at Nymans when the propagation house was built in 1989. The glasshouse guttering channels rainwater from the roof into a galvanized aluminium tank and is then pumped into our irrigation system. Our tanks hold 84,000 litres (22,000 gallons) – all the water we need for the summer. Domestic options range from simple water butts to extensive plastic collection tanks. If we collected and stored all our rain then hosepipe bans would never be neccessary.

Reduced watering

Concerned by the environmental impact of our spectacular but needy summer borders we reviewed their management prior to planting in 2006. Inspired by James Hitchmough and the research of Dr Tijana Blanusa (who have researched systems for more sustainable horticulture and reduced watering), we decided our ornamental bedding would grow in accordance with the amount of water it receives. The traditional, over-watered bedding plant is bloated and poorly adapted to sustain its 'unnatural' bulk. A low-watered plant is a tough individual, less dependent on human intervention. The summer borders in previous years had been watered up to three times a week, during the daytime. We proposed to water once a fortnight, between 6 and 8pm. To reduce the stress of this treatment we applied a 'friendly fungus' inoculant, Trianum–P, after planting and again mid-season.

The result was remarkable – although slightly more compact, the bedding plants produced an excellent display, which rivalled previous years and, as our confidence grew, only received four waterings from May to October. An interesting side effect of the regime was an absence of aphids – our hypothesis being that a lack of soft, sappy growth made the plants much less palatable to them.

Plant selection

An accelerated selection process is taking place in our gardens.
Rhododendrons that have thrived for years struggle through summers,
mature groups of perennial plants wilt and young, previously established trees
fail unless watered. All gardens can do is adapt. We cannot keep plants alive
with constant watering and manipulation of the soil – the best horticulture
should involve the minimum of intervention. Clearly some rhododendrons,
particularly azaleas, are much happier in our changing climate than others.

   New plant selections should be flexible. We chose a *Salvia* x *microphylla*
called 'Hot Lips' for our forecourt garden. From the arid part of the Chiapas
region of Mexico, it thrived in the intense heat of the 2006 summer and
only required an initial watering, while producing a vibrant display of colour.
Interestingly, the plant has been equally happy in the incessant rain of the
2007 summer.

Tip

Try treating trees with a root-dip gel before planting. The 'friendly
fungus' in the gel will help the tree to establish quicker.

Wild-flower meadows

Spirit of the garden

Our old meadows are derived from the principle of hay making, which would have been cut annually for animal fodder on the farm. With the natural setting of the landscape and the interesting qualities of the herbage, this suits the character of the garden particularly well. We have a shallow covering of acidic soil over whinstone rock, which provides just enough nutrients to keep nature's balances in check in a light grass sward that is critical for wild flower survival. Generally we link with what Mother Nature has been doing all her life.

Species rich

We don't plant or put in non-native wild flowers; the meadows are 'native' – rather the plants have chosen to grow there under their own steam. According to the conditions we have let them choose: wet areas encourage the cuckoo pint and the dry, sunny slopes encourage scabious in abundance. Common spotted and butterfly orchids thrive in sunny areas alongside the showy ox-eye daisies while in light shade cowslips, bluebells and violas thrive.

Averil Milligan,
Head Gardener
ROWALLANE
GARDEN, COUNTY
DOWN, NORTHERN
IRELAND

The delightful maturity of this natural garden in County Down, Northern Ireland was planned by Hugh Armytage Moore, from 1903. He had a special eye for plants, placing them within the landscape. The herbage layer is devoted to wild flowers, which flourish among the mature exotics.

Sward maintenance regime

We cut once in autumn after seeding of the wild flowers and grasses has occurred using a pedestrian knife-blade mower (like a hay reaper), which cuts down the sward in one swoop, and like hay making we allow the sward to lie while we finish cutting the area. This can take a few days, which allows the seed to drop out of the harvest back into the ground. When ready to clear the area we attach a 'tedder' to the machine to kick the sward into rows for lifting. The tedding action (like that of a rake) de-thatches the sward as it kicks, allowing light, moisture and seed to drop down into the surface soil to regenerate again. The sward is then taken to make compost after adding various ingredients, but that's another story.

Adding a new area

We have recently added another wild-flower area, the top of which is rich pasture land with lots of vigorous grasses and is unsuitable at the moment to start introductions of wild flowers but we are working on this by taking two cuts off per annum to make it less fertile. In order for wild flowers to survive they must be able to get up through the grasses to sunlight for flowering and seed production, and this would be prevented by lank, thick grass. By cutting and collecting we prevent the enrichment of the sward and will eventually be able to encourage wild flowers to come in; hopefully after some years the seed will blow in itself to establish. At the moment we are monitoring the top sward annually to see when it will be suitable, but it can take a few years and each soil type is different so patience is required. The bottom part is already showing great promise and has common spotted orchids already starting to appear within the second year, so we have adapted the cut to once a year in the lower area accordingly.

Environmentally and labour-friendly gardening

One of the loveliest attributes of a wild-flower meadow is the insect life it encourages. On a sunny day you can sneak up and watch the butterflies feeding from the nectar-rich flowers; the heady sound of bees feeding is extremely restful as they hover above the flowers. Of course, the larger picture brings in all those hidden invertebrates such as the crickets that hide within the sward in their camouflage uniforms, or the earth worm that keeps well out of sight of a hungry thrush. It is wonderful to get down into the sward and listen – the whole area is a factory of activity, with most of it hidden from prying eyes as I discovered when trying to get a photo of that unrecognizable butterfly to look up later...

Of course, the other advantage of managing swards like this is the timing of the work. In a large garden, such as that at Rowallane where the grass needs to be regularly cut regardless of the weather conditions, the wild-flower areas can fit round the weather – a couple of weeks will not make any difference in life's cycle.

Tip

If you are thinking of establishing a meadow either from existing sward or bare earth, consider the soil type, fertility and pH. Examine and look at what is already there or what is wishing to germinate; plants will give you lots of indicators and information.

Index